The Controversy: Godliness vs. Worldliness is an anthology of my eight previously published books. The titles appear in the order they were published, dating back to 1993.

> *Back To Basics*
> *Words Of Wisdom*
> *Words of Wisdom, Too*
> *One Nation Without God*
> *Scripture Servings For Spiritual Strength*
> *Notable Quotables*
> *Matters That Matter, Volume I*
> *Matters That Matter, Volume II*

This publication contains a random, comprehensive selection of related inspirational writings featuring a broad variety of subjects pertaining to life.

Copies of these previously published books are available at:

Fairway Press, 1-800-537-1030 and www.amazon.com

or From the author (see copyright page for address).

THE CONTROVERSY:

Godliness vs. Worldliness

"No one can serve two masters."

Daniel Taddeo

Fairway Press
Lima, Ohio

THE CONTROVERSY

To contact the author, write to:
> Mr. Daniel Taddeo
> 6258 Big Creek Parkway
> Cleveland, Ohio 44130-2288

ISBN-13: 978-0-7880-2227-2
ISBN-10: 0-7880-2227-X

PRINTED IN USA

Dedication

*I would like to dedicate this work
to the restoration and preservation of the family.
It is the very foundation upon which society rests.
It is the first and often the only place
where children learn the right values
to see them through adulthood;
a place where they can be nurtured, loved,
and accepted as God intended.*

Contents

Introduction

Although there are exceptions, most people agree that a universal code of ethics does exist. Any kind of order would be impossible unless all civilized people have a set of principles that determine responsible behavior.

It is inborn for people to appeal to a standard of behavior which they expect others also to understand and follow. "That's not fair" or "How would you like it if someone did that to you?" are thought processes that have no racial or cultural boundaries. C. S. Lewis wrote, "We know that people find themselves under a moral law, which they did not make and cannot quite forget even when they try, and which they know they ought to obey."

Most agree that no society could survive without moral laws that spell out right and wrong conduct. The question then becomes: Whose morality will be legislated? All laws intrude on the morality of someone. Are there moral principles and guidelines that have withstood the unfailing test of time? The answer is yes!

What follows focuses on the subtitle of this book, Godliness vs. Worldliness. Godly truth is determined by God's word: The Ten Commandments. Worldly truth is determined by the culture. Bible truth never changes; it is the same "yesterday and today and forever." Worldly truth is the opposite; it is constantly changing. Whenever these differences are ignored, negative consequences are sure to follow.

Godliness

Just as following natural laws protects people from physical harm, following spiritual laws shields them from much of life's needless suffering and permits them to live meaningful lives. People need moral standards to make good choices. Those who choose a moral code of ethics grounded in the Bible will be well equipped to make all the right moral choices life will ever require. Right moral choices produce positive results and wrong moral choices produce negative results. It's that simple, but not easy.

God cares about every individual ever born. No one is any more or any less valuable or important in His sight. He wants us to view everyone the same way. When we love God, we love others and want what's best for them; and when we love others, we love God.

One might ask, "How do I actually put all of this into practice?" The Bible is very specific about certain rights and wrongs, such as those specified in the Ten Commandments. For those not specifically noted, guiding principles are provided. For example, Micah 6:8 asks and answers the question: "What does the Lord require of you? To act justly and to love mercy and to walk humbly with your God."

James Madison said, "We have staked the whole future of American civilization not upon the power of government, far from it. We have staked the future of all of our political institutions upon the capacity of each and all of us to govern ourselves, to control ourselves, to sustain ourselves according to the Ten Commandments of God."

"There is God's law from which all equitable laws of man emerge and by which men must live if they are not to die in oppression, chaos, and despair" (Cicero 106-43 BC).

Dr. Ron Mehl wrote that God uses them to remove the confusion about right and wrong in today's relativistic culture, protect us from the consequences of our own moral weakness, and guide our thinking and actions in every situation.

Many argue that the Ten Commandments may have been applicable thousands of years ago but certainly not today. They then go on about living their lives their own way. However, popular opinion doesn't make it right. The Decalogue is at the very foundation of our moral code in determining right from wrong conduct. These laws have provided wisdom through the ages and are as applicable today as they were when first given to Moses and the nation of Israel thousands of years before Christ.

The Ten Commandments can be divided into four groups. The first four tell us how to love God. The remaining six tell us how to love our neighbor. "And God spoke all these words saying":

1. YOU SHALL HAVE NO OTHER GODS BEFORE ME. No deity, real or imagined, is to rival the one true god.
2. YOU SHALL NOT MAKE FOR YOURSELF AN IDOL. The worship of false gods such as images, sculptures, statues, and pictures.
3. YOU SHALL NOT TAKE THE NAME OF THE LORD YOUR GOD IN VAIN. Misuse the name of God: curse, desecrate, violate.
4. REMEMBER THE SABBATH DAY BY KEEPING IT HOLY. "Six days you shall work, but the seventh day is a Sabbath to the Lord your God." It was instituted for the benefit of all and it is as equally important as the other nine commandments. Millions of people affiliated with various denominations continue to observe the Sabbath on Saturday, the seventh day of the week, rather than Sunday, the first day of the week.
5. HONOR YOUR FATHER AND YOUR MOTHER. "The first commandment with a promise — that it may go well with you." A fine sense of what is just and right: prize highly, care for, show respect for, and obey. The commandment applies to all family matters: marriage, parenting, children, youth and aging.
6. YOU SHALL NOT MURDER. This commandment forbids the loss of life inflicted by illegal means. Jesus raised this commandment to a new level when He said, "You shall love your neighbor as yourself." When we fail to do this, we commit murder spiritually.
7. YOU SHALL NOT COMMIT ADULTERY. Sexual unfaithfulness of a married person that includes all acts of illicit sex.
8. YOU SHALL NOT STEAL. Take anything without permission that doesn't belong to you.
9. YOU SHALL NOT GIVE FALSE TESTIMONY AGAINST YOUR NEIGHBOR. Disloyal, inaccurate, distort, lie, wrong, untrue, incorrect, intent to deceive.
10. YOU SHALL NOT COVET. Painfully envious of possessions or relationships that belong to others (Exodus 20:3-17).

The Ten Commandments have always served as a strong guide to control violent outbursts in individuals as well as in society.

The answer to America's problems does not lie in more government spending, more laws, more police, or more jails. These actions focus on putting out fires rather than preventing them. What the situation calls for is a return to biblical moral values on which our nation was founded.

Worldliness

Worldly beliefs, principles, and values have been popular in the past, they remain so in the present and will continue to be the case in the future. This doesn't make it right.

Some of the most intelligent and best educated people in America are those selected to the Supreme Court. Most of their decisions have been positive. Others were negative. For example: Black Americans were not citizens, racial discrimination was legal, and women could not vote.

All human inventions, such as traditions, customs, and ceremonies that are contrary to the commandments of God will be found worthless in that day when "God will bring every work into judgment, including every secret thing, whether good or evil" (Ecclesiasties 12:14).

In our culture, we often discover too late that what we thought was right turns out to be wrong and what we thought was wrong turns out to be right. The test for a right decision is: Did it adhere to biblical truth? Though a particular choice may seem right at the time, if biblical standards were ignored, eventually, the foolishness of that choice will become evident with negative consequences sure to follow.

The choice is between Godliness (the narrow way) or worldliness (the broad way). "No one can serve two masters. Either he will hate the one and love the other or he will be devoted to the one and despise the other. You cannot serve both God and mammon [materialism]" (Matthew 6:24). It's like trying to go in two different directions at the same time; you end up going in circles and never reaching your destination.

— Dan Taddeo

Back to Basics

Introduction

Back to Basics speaks to parents about the impact home environment has on children during the pre-school years. If children don't learn certain things during these critical years, they may not learn them at all because the season will have passed them by. Remember, much of what is displayed in adults was learned in childhood before children walk, talk, or attend school. The adult example remains the most dominant force in child development.

Parenting is the greatest challenge most adults will ever face. I once heard a mother remark that her former pressure-filled, full-time job was a cakewalk in comparison to full-time parenthood. Isn't that the truth? In addition to the long hours of physical care for children, being responsible for their moral, spiritual, and emotional needs is an awesome task. However, it can also be one of life's most rewarding experiences when good parenting principles are practiced. What follows is intended to help make this possible.

____*Back to Basics* identifies 61 different areas important to parenting. The reader is told what the topic is, why it's important to parents and children, and suggests how to put the applied principles into practice. Selected Bible passages accompany each topic and serve as the authority. Thought not exhaustive, they're ones I believe parents need to address for successful parenting. They aren't speculative. They're grounded in Scripture. And they have withstood the test of time.

— Dan Taddeo

A random selection arranged alphabetically follows:

Accountability

Children need to understand that God holds them responsible for what they are, for what they have been given, and for what they do with their gifts. That's accountability. "So then each of us shall give account of himself to God." "But I say to you that for every idle (careless) word men may speak, they will give account of it in the day of judgment." Children do not have to try to look and be like everybody else, nor be something or someone they are not. God holds them accountable for what they are. No more, no less. "They will give an account to Him who is ready to judge the living and the dead." The Prophet Daniel put it this way: "... The court was seated, and the books (which contain a complete record of everybody's life on earth) were opened."

Children will learn about accountability from you. This important task is not to be left to others. Children learn right from wrong early in life, but at times they may choose to do wrong anyway. Many think they can do what they want as long as nobody finds out. It should be made very clear to them that God knows their every word, thought, and deed before they do! "... For there is nothing covered that will not be revealed, and hidden that will not be unknown."

Anger

Anger is good for you provided it's the right kind. The Bible talks about two kinds of anger: sinful and righteous. Sinful anger is excessive, uncontrolled rage whose intent is to punish and injure and that's not good. But righteous anger is controlled, thereby able to accomplish good. "Be angry and do not sin...." You can use anger with positive results. "Let no corrupt word proceed out of your mouth, but what is good for necessary edification (instruction) that it may impart grace to the hearers."

Hidden or denied anger may cause serious emotional and physical problems. Unresolved anger may surface in the form of headaches, stomach pains, ulcers, nail-biting, lying, cheating, rebellious school behavior, and high absenteeism, to mention a few. The sooner anger is confronted, the sooner it can be defused. "... Do not let the sun go down on your wrath...." Don't allow it to fester. Identifying the source of anger helps children avoid overreacting.

Children learn how to handle anger by observing their parents. God expresses his wisdom in the following passage: "He who is slow to wrath has great understanding, but he who is impulsive exalts folly." When children get angry, parents should first help them recognize it; second, admit it; third, take responsible action in dealing with it. The best cure for anger is to do an unexpected kindness for the person he or she is angry at. This behavior will say, "I am sorry," better than any words.

Attitude

Attitude dictates our behavior. That's why it's so important to have a good one. "For as he thinks in his heart, so is he...." No matter what the facts or circumstances, we have the choice and power to choose the attitude we take toward those facts and circumstances.

With children, attitude can be even more important than facts. Why? Because it depends on how they perceive the facts. Children with similar makeup and circumstances often see themselves differently. For example: Some feel accepted while others feel rejected; some have high self-esteem while others feel unworthy; some feel appreciated while others do not; some see God as condemning while others see Him as loving, caring, and forgiving. Why?

Parents need to be aware of how their attitudes affect their children. Children tend to adopt their parents' attitudes quite early in life. For example, when parents focus on the negative, children tend to do the same. But when parents look for the positive, children will learn that it is what is expected of them. The environment in which children are reared has so much to do with their attitudes about life.

Parents need to encourage their children to focus on the positive aspects of life. Think good thoughts. Look for the best in others. Always treat others the way they want to be treated. Help them to strive to make others feel better. In so doing, they will feel better about themselves. They need to learn that the full life is experienced in direct proportion to how they give of themselves.

Children's attitudes dictate their actions. If their attitudes are God-centered, they are likely to act positively and responsibly. If they are self-centered, they are likely to act negatively and selfishly.

Blame

The blame game is as old as the Garden of Eden. Can't you just see Adam and Eve pointing fingers at each other and at that grinning serpent? God gave man the freedom to choose. When God confronted him, Adam blamed Eve and Eve blamed the devil and neither accepted responsibility for disobeying God. Not much has changed. We blame friends, parents, home, environment, circumstances — anyone but ourselves.

It's a hard lesson but children must be taught to accept responsibility for their actions rather than blame others. They have to understand that if they commit wrong acts they will suffer the consequences. When they don't accept blame, their destructive behavior can go unchecked and things can go from bad to worse. If you allow kids to place blame, you're setting in motion a vicious circle of behavior.

People who blame are basically insecure, have low self-esteem, and do not really like themselves. This may be the result when children have been excessively criticized and resort to blaming as a means to defending themselves. It is very important that parents avoid disciplining their children in front of others whenever possible. Little good and much harm comes from embarrassing, humiliating, and stripping children of their dignity. "Fathers (and mothers) do not provoke your children, lest they become discouraged."

It is very easy to fall into the trap of making excuses to ratio-
nalize behavior. Resist the temptation to blame and thereby set a
good example for your children. Teach them to accept responsibility for their actions and not resort to making excuses and blaming others. It's a grave injustice to overlook irresponsible behavior in children and bail them out rather than letting them face the
consequences of their actions.

Forgiveness

Forgiveness means to pardon; a matter of letting go of resentment, anger, and deep-seated hatred of others and at times ourselves. Forgiveness frees and heals the forgiver and eventually
the forgiven. Our greatest need after salvation is forgiveness.
Children need to know that Jesus and parents love them and forgive them when they sin. It's also important for you to teach your
children how to forgive others.

Not forgiving is harmful. The medical profession is convinced that emotions, such as anger, hatred, resentment, envy,
and fear are at the root of most physical ailments. Not forgiving
means being imprisoned by the past. Forgiveness frees us from
that past.

Because God freely forgives us, we are asked to forgive others when they wrong us.

"... If you have anything against anyone, forgive him, that
your Father in heaven may also forgive you your trespasses. And
be kind to one another, tenderhearted, forgiving one another,
even as God in Christ forgave you." "Judge not, and you shall not
be judged. Condemn not, and you shall not be condemned.
Forgive, and you will be forgiven. " It is in giving that we
receive.

Forgiveness is a recurring theme in the Bible. When we pray
the Lord's Prayer, "Forgive us our debts (sins) as we forgive our
debtors," we ask God to forgive us according to our forgiveness
of others. The forgiveness we give determines the forgiveness we
receive.

Judging

People who judge others often do it to make themselves look better at the expense of others. God says to hate the sin but love the sinner, regardless of the nature of the sin. It's to be left to God to separate right from wrong. He "will render to each one according to his deeds." "For by your words you will be justified, and by your words you will be condemned.' " He will do this in His own time. All have sinned. All come short of the glory of God. None achieves perfection in this life.

When the scribes and Pharisees pressed Jesus to pass judgment on the woman taken in adultery, Jesus responded in the following way: "... 'He who is without sin among you, let him throw a stone at her first.' When Jesus had raised Himself up and saw no one but the woman, He said to her, 'Woman, where are those accusers of yours? Has no one condemned you?' She said, 'No one, Lord.' And Jesus said to her, 'Neither do I condemn you; go and sin no more.' "

When children give other children the opportunity to learn, grow, and change rather than condemn, they benefit themselves as well as others. "Judge not, and you shall not be judged. Condemn not, and you shall not be condemned. Forgive, and you will be forgiven." Children need to understand that their rewards and punishment in this life and the lifeafter will be based on their conduct and performance in this life.

"There is so much good in the worst of us, and so much bad in the best of us, that it hardly becomes any of us to talk about the rest of us." (Author unknown)

Mistakes

"Hindsight is 20/20," someone once said. So when our children make mistakes, let's help them learn from them. Making mistakes is part of being human. No one is free of them. "For we all stumble in many things." Children learn more from their mistakes than any other method of learning.

Parents should not make children feel fearful of making mistakes. In fact mistakes provide opportunities for them to find better ways of doing things. Good parenting welcomes mistakes because children learn so much from them. Parents need to encourage their children to learn from their mistakes then forget them.

Children learn much from risk-taking, as long as they are not life threatening. They instill confidence, improve decision-making, help children deal with uncertainties, and most importantly, help them develop healthy self-images so necessary for success in school and in life. "Far better is to dare mighty things, to win glorious triumphs, even though checkered by failure, than to take rank with those poor spirits who neither enjoy much nor suffer much, because they live in the gray twilight that knows not victory nor defeat," said Theodore Roosevelt.

Children think parents know everything. We know different. Our mistakes shouldn't be hidden for they can be learning opportunities, too.

Children need to realize that God will not reprimand them for making honest mistakes, especially when they seek His guidance and direction. They need to be told that He promises to forgive and forget all their mistakes when they admit them, accept responsibility for them, do not repeat them, and ask God's forgiveness.

Morality

Moral laws spell out right and wrong behavior. Ethics is the process by which these determinations are made. For the Christian, the process is always God-centered instead of self-centered. "There is a way which seems right to a man, but its end is the way of death." Living a moral life means being in harmony with God. Just as following natural laws protects children from physical harm, following spiritual laws shields them from much of life's sufferings and helps them through unavoidable difficulties.

Children will not always be easily convinced that God's morality is in their best interest. Children need to be reminded "... That all things work together for good to those who love God, to those who are called according to His purpose."

God holds parents responsible for teaching their children right from wrong. "And these words which I command you this day shall be in your heart. You shall teach them diligently to your children, and shall talk of them when you sit in your house, when you walk by the way, when you lie down, and when you rise up." Children instilled with a moral code of ethics grounded in the Bible will be well equipped to make all the right moral choices life will require of them. Every moral principle not followed will result in negative consequences for children, parents, and probably others as well.

Motives

Children need to be taught that God knows what they are thinking before they do. "For the ways of man are before the eyes of the Lord, and He ponders (examines) all his paths." "... For the Lord searches all hearts and understands all the intent of the thoughts...." Children often think they can fool their brothers, sisters, parents, friends, and teachers but they cannot fool God. They will soon learn they only fool themselves.

The Bible teaches that God should be the source of our motivation. Children need to be taught to live as Jesus lived. "Let this mind be in you which was also in Christ Jesus." God knows when they are doing their best and that is all He expects of them. Their actions are to please God first rather than themselves or others. "But when you do a charitable deed, do not let your left hand know what your right hand is doing, that your charitable deed may be in secret; and your Father who sees in secret will Himself reward you openly." Unfortunately, people's actions are often based on what people think rather than on what God thinks. Doing something because it is right is not enough. They insist on the recognition and credit from others as well.

There is no telling how much good could be accomplished in this world if individuals focused on pleasing God rather than people. "Take heed that you do not do your charitable deeds before men, to be seen by them. Otherwise you have no reward from your Father in heaven." "Let nothing be done through selfish ambition or conceit...." Only that which is done for the glory of God will merit His glory and reward.

Neighbors

Since "... God created man in His own image...." each and every human being is of equal value and importance to Him. Children need to be taught to see others in this perspective. Nothing pleases parents more than when others treat their children kindly. God feels the same way. It means wishing and wanting what's best for others. "For all the law is fulfilled in one word, even this: 'you shall love your neighbor as yourself.' "

Children will be held accountable for their behavior toward others, based on their maturity level. It may help to remind them that they will see their neighbors in eternity. When children focus on others instead of themselves, it transforms their lives as well.

Children need to understand that loving their neighbor means practicing biblical principles, such as:

1. Loving others in spite of their faults. God does!
2. Their words should lighten the burdens of others.
3. Building others up rather than tearing them down.
4. Forgiving others and being kind.
5. Considering the need of others at least as important as their own.
6. Loving others as God loves them.
7. Living God-fearing (reverent) lives.
8. Acting in ways that attract rather than drive others away.
9. Treating others as equals.

Even though children may not understand or actually live by these principles, parents should continue to teach them by their words and more importantly, by example.

Patience

Patience is the ability to calmly endure unpleasant situations. Exercising self-control under trying circumstances presents the greatest challenge of all. "... Count it all joy when you fall into various trials, knowing that the testing of your faith produces patience." Being patient means looking beyond present circumstances. We are to dwell on the fact that God is in charge rather than on complaining.

Parents should do everything possible to cultivate patience in their children. The reason it's so important is that impatience is the cause of most unhappiness. Patience should be encouraged when children's wants, needs, and goals are not met immediately. They need to be reminded that each minute, hour, and day that passes brings them closer to the end result.

Children should be reminded that their problems during their lives on earth represent but a moment in time compared to eternity. "... Do not forget this one thing, that with the Lord one day is as a thousand years, and a thousand years as one day." "And let us not grow weary while doing good, for in due season we shall reap if we do not lose heart."

Patient people make the most of their trying times. They maintain a positive outlook. They seek ways to improve the situation. They think of ways to use the waiting time profitably.

Patience promotes peace of mind, good health, and more importantly, glorifies God. Parents need to make every effort possible to instruct their children in the Godly trait of patience.

Praise

Praise is such an important ingredient of successful parenting. It is much more effective in bringing out the best in children than criticism. "Pleasant words are like honeycomb, sweetness to the soul and health to the bones." "Do not withhold good from those to whom it is due, when it is in the power of your hand to do so."

Praise can work wonders. Parents should not just think praise; they should express it in their words and actions. How else can children know and benefit from it? Praise encourages, instills confidence, and has the power to lift children's spirits so they can focus on all the positive aspects of their lives. "A word fitly spoken is like apples of gold in settings of silver."

Praise should greatly outnumber criticism. Criticism reduces self-confidence, so necessary for future success. Sincere praise increases it. Praise, encouragement, and appreciation are needed by all. Everybody can be praised for something.

Pride

Pride is original sin. It is the first of the "seven" deadly sins. It is number one because it leads to every other sin. It is a way of thinking that puts self first and God second. Pride means we deny the true God and appoint ourselves as God. This allows us to put ourselves before others and do whatever is necessary for personal gain at any cost.

Pride destroys. "Pride goes before destruction, and a haughty (arrogant) spirit before a fall." "The Lord will destroy the house of the proud." Recall what happens to King Nebuchadnezzar: "... He was walking about the royal palace of Babylon," he said, "Is not this the great Babylon I have built for a royal residence, by my mighty power and for the honor of my majesty?" While the word was still in the King's mouth, a voice came from heaven: "King Nebuchadnezzar, to you it is spoken the kingdom has departed from you! And they shall drive you from men, and your dwelling shall be with the beast of the field. They shall make you eat grass like oxen." Kings do not have a monopoly on pride. It can get a grip on anyone who pushes God out of his or her life.

The challenge for parents, then, is how to help their children avoid the pit of pride. The psalmist says: "Trust in the Lord with all your heart and lean not on your own understanding; In all your ways acknowledge Him, and He will make your paths straight." Children need to conduct themselves according to what is acceptable to God, not self.

Pride offends God because it degrades individuals who are equally important to Him. Children need to understand that God wants them to build others up and not tear them down. Parents need to show consideration for others and teach their children to do the same. "... God resists the proud but gives grace to the humble." The less proud they are the more they will be able to follow God's will.

Procrastination

Procrastination is needless delay. It's a weakness in our character that prevents us from doing what needs to be done. Often it's something people choose to avoid or escape from because it's distasteful. They tell themselves they'll do it later. Laziness is also part of the problem. Procrastination is a sinful human failing few escape totally.

Anything parents do to minimize procrastination in their children will reap great dividends in their later years. The most unfortunate thing about this habit is all the time that is wasted. Over time, it robs children of their self-respect, mental health, new opportunities, and time that could be devoted to many other useful activities.

Overcoming procrastination is not easy. It leaves a trail of unfinished business wherever it goes. Attempts to justify it include making excuses, apologies, and regrets. People who accomplish much good in their lives can serve as inspiration. They have dealt with the problem and this is what allows them to get so much done. Impressing upon children the importance of time is a good place to begin.

Certain opportunities may occur only once in a lifetime. If they are not seized at that point, they may be lost forever. The odds of this happening with the procrastinator are much greater. Children need to be reminded of God's expectations of them.

Reading

Parents should be selective in what they allow children to read. There are plenty of good books available; but they are harder to find. Reading good books helps children:

1. Build vocabulary and speaking skills.
2. Encourage curiosity and imagination.
3. Develop thinking and reasoning.
4. Sharpen their listening skills.
5. Improve concentration span.
6. Recognize good writing.
7. Succeed in school and life.

When parents devote about ten or fifteen minutes a day reading aloud to their children, they not only achieve the above, but also the personal attention tells them they are valued, appreciated, and loved.

Parents need to impress upon their children, by example, that the Bible is first on the reading list. People could read every book written and still be ignorant; but if they only read the Bible they would be wise. Given the choice, people can get by not having read other books but they wouldn't want to live their lives without knowing about their salvation as revealed in the Bible.

Good reading habits are much more likely to take root in children when reading is an important part of their upbringing. The desire to read, like other meaningful accomplishments, must come from within. Only then will children like it, pursue it, and want to do more of it.

Sin

Sin is a turning away from God. "Whoever commits sin also commits lawlessness, and sin is lawlessness." It is any thought, word, or action that is contrary to God's teachings. It forms a barrier that separates us from God; we want to live our way rather than His way. No one is without sin.... "There is none righteous (without sin). No, not one." "If we say that we have no sin, we deceive ourselves, and the truth is not in us." Only Jesus lived without sin.

Some people concern themselves more with certain sins than others. The "Seven Deadly Sins" in the writings of St. Thomas Aquinas are such an example:

1. Pride — an absorbing sense of one's own greatness often at the expense of others.
2. Avarice — greed; covetousness; excessive desire of gaining and possessing wealth.
3. Lust — extreme desire for pleasure that is selfish and irresponsible.
4. Anger — uncontrolled rage, hostility, revenge, and resentment towards others.
5. Gluttony — excessive eating and drinking to the point of hurting the body.
6. Envy — discontent over another's possessions or good fortune.
7. Sloth — laziness; unwilling to work to the point of using others.

These sins are not listed as such in the Bible. God does not prioritize sin because all sin is deadly in one way or another. They are mentioned here briefly to illustrate a point and will be discussed in greater depth throughout this publication.

Spiritual Birth

At some point all adults as well as children must, of their own free will, decide to accept Jesus as their personal Savior. Then spiritual birth will follow. Jesus says, "... Unless one is born of water and the Spirit, he cannot enter the kingdom of God. That which is born of the flesh is flesh, and that which is born of the Spirit is spirit." The flesh dies but the Spirit lives in eternity.

It's important for parents to know that most people who come to know Christ do so before they are old enough to leave home. Parents should do all they can to influence a spiritual birth but they can't do it all. Jesus says, "No one can come to Me unless the Father who sent Me draws him...." The rebirth experience is a gradual unfolding process that continues throughout life, much like a baby grows into adulthood. Children are not born from above again because their parents are. They must experience this for themselves. Then God opens their eyes to a life with new meaning and purpose.

Children need to be taught they will never understand everything there is to know about God. "... No one can find out the work that God does from beginning to end." It is like each generation painting part of a painting; but no one sees the painting completed. This is the way God intended it to be, but by learning about God in His Holy Word and trusting in His promises, He will become such a power in their lives they will soon learn to do what is right in His sight.

Starting School

Few parents realize how much their children have learned by age six. Gender-identity has been established; they have taken the turn that leads to male or female. They have acquired two-thirds of their height. They will be one-third of the way toward being practically on their own. Some child experts say that by age six children learn over half of what they will ever know. Most of the seeds that determine behavior will have been planted. The kinds of fruit they will bear, during the next twelve years and the rest of their lives, will come from these seeds.

Allowing children to start school before they are ready often leads to a continuous struggle of playing "catch up." In many instances, it means the difference between liking or hating school. Three out of four younger boys and one out of four younger girls encounter serious difficulties at school.

My recommendation is that children who turn six in June or later of that year (five for kindergarten) should not enroll in first grade that September, but rather wait until the following September. These children will be seven (six for kindergarten) when they start school. This means that all first graders will be seven years old by the end of the school year. Keeping summer birthday children out of school until the following year will allow the children to reach age eighteen before high school graduation rather than after. When in doubt, starting school later is better than starting earlier.

Talent

Children can easily be made to feel inadequate if denied the biblical point of view regarding talent. The Bible teaches that every human being has an important place in God's kingdom. Children differ physically, mentally, and emotionally. One of the greatest gifts parents can give their children is to help them identify their unique talents. Nurturing and motivating them in those talents not only pleases them, it pleases God.

God's expectations never exceed a child's gifts and talents. Children are responsible for only what God has endowed them. It's very comforting for children, and adults also, to know that they don't have to be like everybody else.

God in His divine wisdom and love did not make us all alike. He made some more talented than others as illustrated in the parable of the talents. "And to one He gave five talents, to another two, and to another one, to each according to his own ability...." The one who had received five talents traded with them and made another five talents. He who had received two gained two more, also. He who had received one went and dug in the ground and hid his lord's money. The two servants who doubled their five and two talents were praised equally by their master. The one who had hid and returned his one talent was condemned by his master and even that was taken from him.

Parents should encourage their children to thank God and praise Him for their many blessings, their time, talents, abilities, and tangible goods. Ask His guidance in using them to advance His kingdom and to glorify His name to the best of their ability.

Television

Television is one of the greatest inventions of all time. Since the 1950s it has affected peoples' lives more than any other technological development. For the first time in history something other than parents has become the main provider of information, values, and entertainment for children. Television has changed how the family functions, how people think, what they buy, how they dress, and what they do during their free time.

Surveys tell us that average pre-school age children, ages 2 to 5, spend a third or more of their total waking hours watching TV. Most children will spend more time watching TV than any other single activity during the first eighteen years of their lives except sleep. It can rob adults of their moral and spiritual values and cripple their emotional and physical development.

Television programming is saturated with violence, sex, distorted role models, trivia, and immorality. In addition to all of the above and more, TV viewing is extremely passive. Children put little into it; therefore, they get little value out of it. Plus, they've wasted valuable time that could be put to better use.

According to the American Academy of Pediatrics, children should be limited to watching no more than two hours of TV a day. It helps to decide ahead of time the programs to watch. Having only one TV in the home will help to achieve this goal.

Temptation

Temptation is anything that lures or entices us to act outside of God's will. It's not a sin to be tempted but it is sinful to yield to it. "Let no one say when he is tempted, 'I am tempted of God'; for God cannot be tempted by evil, nor does He Himself tempt anyone. But each one is tempted when he is drawn away by his own desires and enticed. Then when desire has conceived it gives birth to sin; and sin, when it is full-grown, brings forth death."

When children find themselves tempted to act outside God's will, parents should encourage them to ask: What would happen if I yielded? Would it be worth the consequences? They should be honest in thinking through the outcome. Ask God for strength to resist temptation. "Watch and pray, lest you enter into temptation. The spirit indeed is willing, but the flesh is weak."

"No temptation has overtaken you except such as in common to man; but God is faithful, who will not allow you to be tempted beyond what you are able, but with the temptation will also make the way of escape, that you may be able to bear it." "Blessed is the man who endures temptation; for when he has been approved, he will receive the crown of life which the Lord has promised to those who love Him." By trusting in what God says is right and doing what God would have them do, children can be assured that God's grace will be there to help them resist temptation where and when they need it.

Truth

Truthfulness is a character trait that needs to be instilled very early in children. They will face many opportunities when they will be tempted to avoid or turn from the truth because of the cost involved. It's important they decide in advance how they will react when such occasions arise. They may find it hard to do at first but such experiences help them stand for what is right when there's pressure from their peers to compromise their integrity.

Parents, by example, can best teach their children the principles of truthfulness. It is at this junction in their young lives that they decide which fork in the road they will take. The road of God's truth or the road of self-truth. "Therefore putting away lying, 'let each one of you speak truth with his neighbor,' for we are members of one another." "Buy the truth, and do not sell it, also wisdom and instruction and understanding." "... God our savior desires all men to be saved and to come to the knowledge of the truth." This acquired truth allows God to be in charge of our lives.

One of God's most exciting promises is found in John's gospel where Jesus said, "If you abide in My word, you are My disciples indeed. And you shall know the truth and the truth shall make you free." Freedom from the weaknesses of human nature. Freedom from thoughts, words, and actions that hurt and destroy self and others. Freedom from earthly sin that leads to eternal death. This acquired freedom allows God to direct our lives so we can reap His many blessings.

Values

There is a growing trend in the thinking that anything goes. There is no right and wrong. It's happening in many homes, schools, government, and society in general: devotion to God, honesty, tolerance, respect, and ethical behavior are just a few of the traditional values eroding around us. A growing number of people are interested only in fulfilling their own desires. "There is a way that seems right to a man, but its end is the way of death."

Are there true basic values that will serve everyone under all circumstances and at all times? Christianity teaches that there are. "Trust in the Lord with all your heart, and lean not on your own understanding. In all your ways acknowledge Him, and He shall direct your path." The ultimate test is whether values are constructive or destructive.

Children learn their values from parents. Parents' values become their children's values. They unconsciously absorb them from birth on. The values children adopt before they go to school will be a major factor in how they will do in school and life. If they have been instilled with such basic values as respect for authority, self-discipline, and obedience, they will learn and benefit from what school has to offer.

Children need to know that the Bible is the one place they can go for dependable help when trying to decide right from wrong and this applies to all people, all the time, and under all circumstances.

Worldliness

The Scripture has much to say about worldliness. Following is a selection of those passages. Jesus said we are to be mindful of the things of God not of the world. "For what will it profit a man if he gains the whole world and loses his soul...?" "Do you not know that friendship with the world is enmity with God? Whoever therefore wants to be a friend of the world makes himself an enemy of God." "For where your treasure is, there your heart will be also."

Children need to be taught that the only thing they can count on with certainty in this world is God because everything else is constantly changing.

Jesus teaches that materialism apart from God leads to destruction. Most people in many ways live opposite of what God intended. They will need to prepare for the fact that as Christians, they will face opposition and criticism. God-fearing people have always been and will continue to be in the minority.

Children need to be taught what it means for them to be in the world but not of it. That God's standards should influence the world and not the other way around. "Set your mind on things above, not on things on the earth." "He who loves his life (puts God second) will lose it, and he who hates his life (puts God first) in this world will keep it for eternal life."

"Let your conduct be without covetousness; be content with such things as you have." Children are to strive for behavior that pleases God.

Words of Wisdom

Introduction

The purpose of this section is to share with the reader what some of the greatest thinkers have to say about life. Their words of wisdom have inspired and continue to inspire people the world over.

— Dan Taddeo

A random selection arranged alphabetically follows:

Commandments of Human Relations

1. Speak to people. There is nothing as nice as a cheerful word of greeting.

2. Smile at people. It takes 72 muscles to frown and only 14 to smile.

3. Call people by name. The sweetest music to many ears is the sound of one's own name.

4. Be friendly and helpful. If you would have friends, be friendly.

5. Be cordial. Speak and act as though everything you do is pleasurable.

6. Have a genuine interest in people. People like to be noticed and appreciated.

7. Be generous with praise, be cautious with criticism. Overcome them with goodness.

8. Be considerate of the feelings of others. Try walking in their shoes.

9. Be thoughtful of the opinions of others. Respect their viewpoints.

10. Be alert to give service. What counts most in life is what we do for others.

— Anonymous

Desiderata

Go placidly amid the noise and the haste, and remember what peace there may be in silence.

As far as possible without surrender be on good terms with all persons.

Speak your truth quietly and clearly; and listen to others, even the dull and ignorant; they too have their story.

Enjoy your achievements as well as your plans.

Keep interested in your own career, however humble; it is a real possession in the changing fortunes of time.

Be yourself.

Take kindly the counsel of years, gracefully surrendering the things of youth.

Nurture strength of spirit to shield you in sudden misfortune.

But do not distress yourself with imaginings. Many fears are born of fatigue and loneliness.

You are a child of the universe no less than the trees and the stars; you have a right to be here.

And whether or not it is clear to you, no doubt the universe is unfolding as it should.

Therefore be at peace with God, whatever you conceive Him to be;

And whatever your labors and aspirations, in the noisy confusion of life, keep peace with your soul.

With all its sham, drudgery and broken dreams, it is still a beautiful world. Be careful.

Strive to be happy.

— Found in old Saint Paul's Church, Baltimore, dated 1692

Friends

Friends are special people we admire and hold in high esteem. They help us to live better lives, and we all need them. Children are no exception. Adults and children alike can get so desperate for friendship they even try to buy it in an effort to avoid rejection. Parents need to teach their children that in order to have friends they must be one themselves. Children need to ask themselves how they would want their friends to think of them. Then get on with doing it. Here are some specific actions they can take:

1. Loving. "A new commandment I give to you, that you love one another; as I have loved you, that you also love one another." "Greater love has no one than this, to lay down one's life for his friends."
2. Friendliness. "A man who has friends must himself be friendly...."
3. Persistence. "A friend loves at all times."
4. Loyalty. "Do not forsake your own friend...."
5. Peacemaking. "... Let us pursue the things which make for peace and the things by which one may edify another."
6. Sincerity. "Let each of you look out not only for his own interests, but also for the interests of others."

The list of qualities for being a friend is endless. Children should be taught that friendship just doesn't happen. Seeds have to be planted and cultivated. They have to work at it. Friendship is built more on giving and less on taking. Emphasis should always be more on being a friend rather than finding one.

Everyone needs at least one good friend. Fortunately, everyone is guaranteed one. That person is Jesus. It is reassuring to know that if their earthly friends let them down, children will still always have Jesus as their friend. He will never let them down. He knows all about them and loves them just as they are. He understands everything about them and promises to be their friend forever.

Giving

Giving is something that doesn't come easily to most people. Human nature leans much toward receiving than giving. This attitude changes only when we understand that giving benefits the giver more than the receiver. "For it is in giving that we receive."

Jesus gave His life. Most of us are only expected to give some of our time or our talents or our treasures, which are all God-given. The Bible says that giving always leaves us with more, not less. "One man gives freely, yet gains even more; He who refreshes others will himself be refreshed." "He who sows bountifully will also reap bountifully."

When it comes to giving, a few people always put themselves first; a few always put others first; all the rest of us fall somewhere in between. To grow in giving, every person needs to ask: Where do I fall on this continuum of giving? On those occasions when I'm able to put others first, the passage, "It is more blessed to give than to receive," always rings true! Unfortunately, it also happens to be one of the least practiced messages in all of the Bible.

Happiness

Happiness is a funny thing. You can't see it or hear it or touch it and no one has ever really defined it. But those who possess it treasure it and those who don't, often spend their lives searching for it.

Happiness comes, not from receiving, but from giving of love, of sympathy, of faith, of understanding. And, oddly enough, the more we give, the happier we become and the happier we become, the more we have to give.

Happiness is a state of mind that depends entirely on you. We talk of others "making us happy," but this is seldom the case. We make ourselves happy or unhappy by our attitudes toward ourselves, our work, our neighbors, our world.

The truly happy person is one who can be enthusiastic about the things he has to do as well as the things he wants to do.

Happiness is a wonderful thing. It is the one gift we can give ourselves — and the most precious gift that we can wish for.

— Anonymous

Healthy Challenges

Heed not the worst in a person, seek out and love what is the best in him.

Apply yourself to every task as if it were the only occupation in the world.

Prayer is the protein of the Spiritual life. It is the nourishment without which actions and

Good words wither away and die.

Pollution of the Soul by sin can be purified by God; just ask for His help.

Invest your mind and your interests as you would your money, in worthwhile activities that will reap long dividends.

Nourish Hope. Hope is the flame that enkindles our fire which casts out darkness.

Each day begins with this thought: "Today is the beginning of the rest of my life!"

Success is measured by endeavor. The only real failure is the man who does not try.

Share your happy day with someone. It will mean more to him and to you.

— Anonymous

Jesus

The moral and spiritual values born out of His Word provide the foundation for sound character and good citizenship. Jesus reveals Himself in the following "I AM" statements as recorded in John's gospel.

"I AM the bread of life. He who comes to me shall never hunger, and he who believes in me shall never thirst."

"I AM the light of the world. He who follows me shall not walk in darkness, but have the light of life."

"I AM the door. If anyone enters by me, he will be saved."

"I AM the good shepherd. The good shepherd gives his life for the sheep."

"I AM the resurrection and the life. He who believes in me, though he may die, he shall live."

"I AM the way, the truth, and the life. No one comes to the Father except through me."

"I AM the vine; you are the branches. He who abides in me, and I in him, bears much fruit; for without me you can do nothing."

The Lord's Prayer

OUR FATHER IN HEAVEN... "Give thanks to the Lord."

HALLOWED BE YOUR NAME... "For the Lord is great and greatly to be praised."

YOUR KINGDOM COME... "The Kingdom of God is within you."

YOUR WILL BE DONE ON EARTH AS IT IS IN HEAVEN... "If we ask anything according to his will, He hears us."

GIVE US THIS DAY OUR DAILY BREAD... "Present your requests to God."

AND FORGIVE US OUR DEBTS AS WE FORGIVE OUR DEBTORS... "If you do not forgive, neither will your Father in heaven forgive your trespasses."

AND DO NOT LEAD US INTO TEMPTATION... "Pray that you may not enter into temptation."

BUT DELIVER US FROM THE EVIL ONE... "I can do all things through Christ who strengthens me."

FOR YOURS IS THE KINGDOM AND THE POWER AND THE GLORY FOREVER... "Blessed be the name of God."

AMEN... "It shall be so."

— Matthew 6:9-13

I Loved You Enough...

Some day when my children are old enough to understand the logic that motivates a mother, I will tell them:

I loved you enough to ask where you were going, with whom, and what time you would be home.

I loved you enough to insist that you save your money and buy a bike for yourself even though we could afford to buy one for you.

I loved you enough to make you take a Milky Way back to the drugstore (with a bite out of it) and tell the clerk, "I stole this yesterday and want to pay for it."

I loved you enough to stand over you for two hours while you cleaned your room, a job that would have taken me fifteen minutes.

I loved you enough to let you see anger, disappointment, and tears in my eyes. Children must learn that their parents are not perfect.

I loved you enough to let you assume that responsibility for your actions even when the penalties were so harsh they almost broke my heart.

But most of all, I loved you enough to say NO when I knew you would hate me for it. Those were the most difficult battles of all. I am glad I won them because in the end you won something, too.

— Anonymous

My Favorite Bible Quotations

"Give, and it will be given to you.... For with the same measure that you use, it will be measured back to you." (Luke 6:38)

"Those who wait on the Lord shall renew their strength; they shall mount up with wings like eagles, they shall run and not be weary, they shall walk and not faint" (Isaiah 40:31).

"This is the day the Lord has made; we will rejoice and be glad in it" (Psalm 118:24).

"Unless the Lord builds the house, they labor in vain who build it" (Psalm 127:1).

"Let no corrupt word proceed out of your mouth, but what is good for necessary edification, that it may impart grace to the hearers" (Ephesians 4:29).

"If God is for us, who can be against us?" (Romans 8:31).

"I can do all things through Christ who strengthens me" (Philippians 4:13).

"The things which are impossible with men are possible with God" (Luke 18:27).

"Whatever you want men to do to you, do also to them...." (Matthew 7:12).

"For God so loved the world that He gave His only begotten Son, that whoever believes in Him should not perish but have everlasting life" (John 3:16).

"And what does the Lord require of you? To act justly, and to love mercy and to walk humbly with your God" (Micah 6:8).

"For what will it profit a man if he gains the whole world and loses his own soul" (Mark 8:36).

"For where your treasure is, there your heart will be also" (Matthew 6:21).

"Though the fig tree does not bud and there are no grapes on the vine, though the olive crop fails and the fields produce no food, though there are no sheep in the pen and no cattle in the stalls, yet I will rejoice in the Lord, I will be joyful in God my savior" (Habakkuk 3:17-18).

Priorities

1. Spiritual: "You shall love the Lord your God with all your heart, with all your soul, and with all your strength."

2. Family: "Choose for yourself this day whom you will serve... But as for me and my house, we will serve the Lord."

3. Neighbors: "You shall love your neighbor as yourself."

4. Health: "Do you not know that your body is the temple of the Holy Spirit who is in you, whom you have from God, and you are not your own?"

5. Work: "And whatever you do, do it heartily, as to the Lord and not to men."

6. Education: "You shall teach them [God's Laws] diligently to your children, and shall talk of them when you sit in your house, when you walk by the way, when you lie down, and when you rise up."

7. Money: "For the love of money is the root of all kinds of evil."

8. Material Comforts: "Seek the kingdom of God, and all these things shall be added to you."

Salvation

Salvation is our greatest need. The Bible teaches that spiritual birth must follow physical birth. "Unless one is born again, he cannot see the kingdom of God" (John 3:3). The choice of spiritual birth is then followed by a gradual growth process that continues throughout life, much like a baby matures to adulthood.

God gives us the only plan for salvation in His Word:

1. Admit we are sinners: "For all have sinned and fall short of the glory of God" (Romans 3:23). Sin separates us from God. To escape sin's penalty, we need divine forgiveness. It's ours through faith and trust in Jesus.

2. Believe that Jesus, God in the flesh, died on the cross to pay the penalty for our sins and trust Him for our salvation. "Believe on the Lord Jesus Christ, and you will be saved" (Acts 16:31).
3. Commit ourselves to obeying God's word. "Therefore, if anyone is in Christ, he is a new creation; old things have passed away; behold all things have become new" (2 Corinthians 5:17).

Lord, Jesus, I know I am a sinner and need your forgiveness. I believe you died for my sins. I want to turn from my sins. I now invite you to come into my heart and life. I want to trust and follow you as Lord and Savior. In Thy name I pray. Amen.

Twenty-Third Psalm

The Lord is my Shepherd. I shall not want; He maketh me to lie down in green pastures. He leadeth me beside the still waters; He restoreth my soul. He leadeth me in the paths of righteousness for his name's sake. Yea, though I walk through the valley of the shadow of death, I will fear no evil; for thou art with me; they rod and thy staff, they comfort me. Thou preparest a table before me in the presence of mine enemies; thou anointest my head with oil; my cup runneth over. Surely goodness and mercy shall follow me all the days of my life; and I will dwell in the house of the Lord for ever.

Waste

Waste has become one of the most critical issues in today's society. But waste does more than fill up our trash cans. It is the useless expenditure of time, money, effort, talent, and other valuable resources. It's what is squandered after our needs are met. It's carelessness, it's thoughtlessness, it's irresponsible behavior.

Use what you need but don't deny others through waste. "If anyone has material possessions and sees his brother in need but has no pity on him, how can the love of God be in him?" (1 John 3:17).

Children learn wasteful or conserving habits from their parents' example. For example, energy experts say that we waste as much energy as we really need because lights, appliances, and water are not turned off. There are many ways of preventing waste. As minor as they may seem, it can really add up when millions of people pull together. Waste is sinful because others suffer as a result of it. Children need to be taught to think about the welfare of others and not just their own.

Think about the impact that New England saying could have in the world: "Use it up, wear it out, make it do, or do without."

Whatever Became of Sin?

Sin is the transgression of God's law. Even though psychiatrists have assigned other names to these transgressions, the fact remains that when God's law is broken someone is violated. Someone is offended. Someone is injured. Sin by any other name is still sin and the consequences are the same.

The following is a partial summary of cultural trends in America's society based on a comparison of information extracted from The US Census.

1. Crime: violent crime has escalated over 300%.
2. Education: significant drop in test scores.
3. Drugs and Alcohol: consumption up dramatically.
4. Television: average family watches 49 hours per week, most of which is negative.
5. Sex: five times the number of illegitimate births.
6. Attitude: self-control giving way to self-expression.
7. Family: three times the number of children in single-parent homes. Dramatic increase in divorce, poverty, child abuse, abortion, disobedience, juvenile arrests, and teen suicide.

This kind of behavior has dulled the distinction between right and wrong in America today. Our society is moving from one whose values were primarily spiritual and moral to one whose values are becoming more materialistic and immoral.

"All we like sheep have gone astray: we have turned, every one, to his own way" (Isaiah 53:6).

You Will Never Be Sorry

For hearing before judging,
For forgiving your enemies,
For being candid and frank,
For helping a fallen brother,
For being honest in business,
For thinking before speaking,
For being loyal to your church,
For standing by your principles,
For stopping your ears to gossip,
For bridling a slanderous tongue,
For harboring only pure thoughts,
For sympathizing with the afflicted,
For being courteous and kind to all.

— Anonymous

Words of Wisdom, Too

Introduction

The purpose of this section is to share what some of the wisest thinkers have to say about life. Their words of wisdom have inspired people the world over.

These 244 selections that appear in this section are far from exhaustive. They have appealed to me over years as praiseworthy thoughts that are instrumental in the development of the American character.

There is something for everyone — inspirational messages that have come down to us since the dawn of history which serve to enrich the quality of life.

— Dan Taddeo

A random selection arranged alphabetically follows:

Believe

"I believe in the greatness of the individual, and that I am in this world for a purpose, that purpose being to put back into life more than I have taken out.

"I believe in the integrity of other people, assured that they try as hard to follow the gleam, even as I.

"I believe in the gallantry of older people whose seasoned experienced and steadfast devotion has preserved for me the precious heritage of the past.

"I believe in the magnificence of the past, knowing that without its storied wealth I would possess nothing.

"I believe in the challenge of the future, fully realizing there will be no future except it becomes alive through me.

"I believe in the contagion of health, and that I can spread it through cheerfulness, wholesome habits, sensible expenditure of energies, and wise use of foods.

"I believe in the nobility of work as the creative expression of the best within me and as my share in easing the common load of all.

"I believe in the enrichment of play and laughter as the means of cleansing my body of staleness and my soul of bitterness.

"I believe in God, who justifies all these beliefs; He is the still small voice within, ever urging me toward the unattained. Since He cares for these things, I believe that even death cannot steal these precious possessions from me.

"And whatever more I believe is entwined in those precious feelings that lie too deep for words."

What a person believes has everything to do with what a person becomes.

— Anonymous

Contentment

Our pursuit of contentment (happiness) is the driving force in most all we do. There's no limit to the sacrifices we make and the pain we endure to gain it. We want it so much that we spend our whole life in search of it.

What is contentment? It's the state of being satisfied with what we have. It's not wealth. It's not material possessions. It's not circumstances, and it's not security. The world is filled with disappointed people seeking contentment in these and other ways. Material comforts, conveniences, and desires can accompany contentment, but they don't guarantee it. How do we know? Because millions of people have all these things and are not content; and there are many people who possess little, who are content.

The world would have us believe that acquiring things for ourselves leads to happiness, but the Bible teaches just the opposite. "It is more blessed to give than to receive." Therefore, Christ's teaching encourages us to think of other's needs, and to give, serve, and share. In these actions we will receive joy, inward peace, and contentment.

The apostle Paul wrote, "I have learned to be content whatever the circumstances. I know what it means to be in need, and I know what it is to have plenty. I have learned the secret of being content in any and every situation, whether well fed or hungry, whether living in plenty or in want. I can do everything through him who gives me strength" (Philippians 4:11-13). Contentment is found in God not self.

— Dan Taddeo

Don't Quit

When things go wrong, as they sometimes will,
When the road you're trudging seems all uphill,
When the funds are low and the debts are high,
And you want to smile, but you have to sigh,
When care is pressing you down a bit —
Rest if you must, but don't you quit.

Life is queer with its twist and turns,
As every one of us sometimes learns,
And many a fellow turns about
When he might have won had he stuck it out.
Don't give up though the peace seems slow —
You may succeed with another bow.

Often the goal is nearer than
It seems to a faint and faltering man;
Often the struggler has given up
When he might have captured the victor's cup;
And he learned too late when the night came down,
How close he was to the golden crown.

Success is failure turned inside out —
The silver tint of the clouds of doubt,
And you never can tell how close you are,
It may be near when it seems afar;
So stick to the fight when you're hardest hit,
It's when things seem worst that you mustn't quit.

— Anonymous

Educated Man

Whom do I call educated? First, those who manage well the circumstances which they encounter day by day and those who possess a judgment which is accurate in meeting occasions as they arise and rarely miss the expedient course of action.

Next, those who are decent and honorable in their intercourse with all men, bearing easily and good naturedly what is unpleasant and offensive to others, and being as agreeable and reasonable to their associates as it is humanly possible to be.

Furthermore, those who hold their pleasures always under control and are not ultimately overcome by their misfortunes, bearing up under them bravely and in a manner worthy of our common nature.

Finally, and most important of all, those who are not spoiled by their successes, who do not desert their true selves, but hold their ground steadfastly as wise and sober-minded men, rejoicing no more in the good things that have come to them through chance than in those which, through their own nature and intelligence, are theirs since birth.

Those who have a character which is in accord, not with one of these things, but with all of them — these I maintain are educated and whole men possessed of all the virtues of a man.

— Socrates, 468-399 BC

Footprints in the Sand

One night a man had a dream. He dreamed he was walking along the beach with the Lord. Across the sky flashed scenes from his life. For each scene, he noticed two sets of footprints in the sand: one belonging to him, and the other to the Lord. When the last scene of his life flashed before him, he looked back at the footprints in the sand. He noticed that many times along the path of his life there was only one set of footprints. He also noticed that it happened at the very lowest and saddest times in his life.

This really bothered him and he questioned the Lord about it. "Lord, You said that once I decided to follow you, You'd walk with me all the way. But I have noticed that during the most troublesome times in my life, there is only one set of footprints. I don't understand why when I needed you most you would leave me." The Lord replied, "My son, My precious child, I love you and I would never leave you. During your times of trial and suffering, when you see only one set of footprints, it was then that I carried you."

— author unknown

Forgive Me When I Whine

Today, upon the bus I saw a lovely girl with golden hair,
I envied her, she seemed so gay, and I wished I were so fair.
When suddenly she rose to leave, and I saw her hobble down the aisle.
She had one leg, and wore a crutch and, as she passed, a smile.

Oh, God, forgive me when I whine... I have two legs. The world is mine.

And then I stopped to buy some sweets, the lad who sold them had such charm.
I talked to him; he seemed so glad if I were late 'twould do no harm.
And as I left he said to me: "Thank you. You have been so kind.
It's nice to talk to folks like you. You see," he said, "I'm blind."

Oh, God, forgive me when I whine... I have two eyes. The world is mine.

Later, walking down the street, I saw a child with eyes of blue.
He stood and watched the others play. It seemed he knew not what to do.

I stopped a moment, then I said, "Why don't you join the others, dear?"

He looked ahead without a word, and then I knew he could not hear.

Oh, God, forgive me when I whine... I have two ears. The world is mine.

With legs to take me where I'd go, with eyes to see the sunset glow,
two ears to hear what I would know...

Oh, God, forgive me when I whine... I'm blessed indeed. The world is mine.

— Anonymous

Gettysburg Address

Four score and seven years ago our fathers brought forth on this continent a new nation conceived in liberty and dedicated to the proposition that all men are created equal.

Now we are engaged in a great civil war testing whether our nation or any nation so conceived and so dedicated can long endure. We are met on a great battlefield of that war. We have come to dedicate a portion of that field as a final resting place for those who here gave their lives that that nation might live. It is altogether fitting and proper that we should do this. But in a large sense we cannot dedicate — we cannot consecrate — we cannot hallow this ground. The brave men living and dead who struggled here have consecrated it far above our poor power to add or detract.

The world will little note nor long remember what we say here but it can never forget what they did here. It is for us the living rather to be dedicated here to the unfinished work which they who fought here have thus far so nobly advanced. It is rather for us to be here dedicated to the great task remaining before us that from these honored dead we take increased devotion to that cause for which they gave the last full measure of devotion. That we here highly resolve that these dead shall not have died in vain. That this nation under God shall have a new birth of freedom. And that government of the people by the people for the people shall not perish from the earth.

— Abraham Lincoln

Gossip

An unknown author had this to say on the subject: "My name is Gossip. I have no respect for justice; I ruin without killing; I tear down homes; I break hearts and wreck lives. I am wily, cunning, malicious, and I gather strength with age. I make my way where greed, mistrust, and dishonor are unknown. I feed on good and bad alike. My victims are as numerous as the sands of the sea, and often as innocent. I never forgive and seldom forget. My name is Gossip."

Man was created by God to live and work with his fellow man, not to hurt him; to build up, not tear down; to draw people together in love, not to separate them by strife.

If we catch in flight the impulse to be unkind and change it to a charitable word or action, we would make a big difference in the world. Isn't it worth the effort?

"Keep your tongue from evil, and your lips from speaking deceit" (Psalm 34:13).

Guiding Principles

1. I need to be more sensitive to others and not offend them, judge them, or cause them to stumble.
2. I need to be more intentional about how I live among others, not alienating them needlessly, doing what upbuilds and leads to peace.
3. I need to let God's Word set my standards, not what other people think or do.
4. I need to ask what pleases God, not what pleases those people who don't care about Him. Such, I may lose some relationships.
5. I need to apply my convictions to others gracefully and not arrogantly; I need to say "no" without trumpeting or defending myself; and I need to approach unbelievers and the unchurched more gently.
6. I need to do more things that show my love for God and my fellowman.
7. I need to practice more self-control and self-discipline in my behavior.
8. I need to be more courageous and risk more in approaching unbelievers and the unchurched, as Jesus did.
9. The people farthest from the Gospel will least appreciate the Great Commission: "Go therefore and make disciples of all the nations...."
10. I need to be a more personal and truthful witness, telling what I have learned and experienced about Christ in my own life.

— Anonymous

Here and Now

In our culture, all of us are preoccupied most of the time with anticipating the future and worrying about it or with daydreaming about the past and remembering how it was. We are always trying to be happier right now, and yet much of what we do prevents us from achieving that happiness.

To be in the here and now means to be in touch with your senses, to be aware of what you are seeing, hearing, smelling, and so on. Young children find it very easy to be in the here and now, and if you watch them play, you notice that they seldom worry about what is going to happen even an hour or two hours from now and that they spend little time reminiscing. They are concerned with the present situation and with getting the most from it.

If, as teenagers and adults, we could be more like young children, many of the problems that bother us would disappear.

Think about how many nights you weren't able to get to sleep because you were thinking about the future or the past, how many hours of the day you wasted, and how many opportunities you have missed by not allowing your mind and body to experience what is happening now. There is a saying, "The future is only a dream and the past no longer exists. The present moment is the only reality."

— Dan Taddeo

Hope

Hope looks for the good in people instead of harping on the worst.

Hope opens doors where despair closes them.

Hope discovers what can be done instead of grumbling about what cannot.

Hope draws its power from a deep trust in God and the basic goodness of mankind.

Hope "lights a candle" instead of "cursing the darkness."

Hope regards problems, small or large, as opportunities.

Hope cherishes no illusions, nor does it yield to cynicism.

Hope sets big goals and is not frustrated by repeated difficulties and setbacks.

Hope pushes ahead when it would be easy to quit.

Hope puts up with modest gains, realizing that "the longest journey starts with one step."

Hope accepts misunderstandings as the price for serving the greater good of others.

Hope is a good loser because it has the divine assurance of final victory.

— Father James Keller

Hugs

It's wondrous what a hug can do.
A hug can cheer you when you're blue.
A hug can say, "I love you so" or
"Gee, I hate to see you go."

A hug is "Welcome back again!"
And "Great to see you!" or
"Where've you been?"

Hugs are great for fathers and mothers,
Sweet for sisters, swell for brothers.
And chances are some favorite aunts
Love them more than potted plants.

Kittens crave them, puppies love them.
Heads of state are not above them.
A hug can break the language barrier
And make the dullest day seem merrier.

No need to fret about the store of 'em.
The more you give, the more there are of 'em.
So stretch those arms without delay
And give someone a hug today.

— Anonymous

Just For Today

Just for today, I will be as friendly as I can to the people I work with. I will treat them as if they are responsible for keeping me in my job and I'll be grateful they are there.

Just for today, I won't assume my job is to be chief critic. I will try to see the good in every situation, and I will look for something to praise in every person who works with me.

Just for today, if I correct someone, I will do it with as much good humor and self-restraint as if I were the one being corrected.

Just for today, I will feel happy I am at work, alive, and well.

Just for today, I will not have any expectations about how I should be treated, and I will not compare myself with anyone else. I will just be glad that I am who I am.

Just for today, I will not worry about "what's in it for me." I will only think about what I can do to help out in every situation.

Just for today, when I leave work, I will not dwell on how much I did or did not get done. Instead, I will look forward to the evening and be thankful for whatever I accomplish.

— Anonymous

Love

If I speak in the tongues of men and of angels, but I have not love, I am only a resounding gong or a clanging cymbal. If I have the gift of prophecy and can fathom all mysteries and all knowledge, and if I have a faith that can move mountains, but have not love, I am nothing. If I give all I possess to the poor and surrender my body to the flames, but have not love, I gain nothing.

Love is patient, love is kind. It does not envy, it does not boast, it is not proud. It is not rude, it is not self-seeking, it is not easily angered, it keeps no record of wrongs. Love does not delight in evil but rejoices with the truth. It always protects, always trusts, always hopes, always perseveres.

Love never fails. But where there are prophecies, they will cease; where there are tongues, they will be stilled; where there is knowledge, it will pass away. For we know in part and we prophesy in part, but when perfection comes, the imperfect disappears.

When I was a child, I talked like a child, I thought like a child, I reasoned like a child. When I became a man, I put childish ways behind me. Now we see but a poor reflection as in a mirror; then we shall see face to face. Now I know in part; then I shall know fully, even as I am fully known.

And now these there remain: faith, hope and love. But the greatest of these is love.

— 1 Corinthians 13:1-13

My Favorite Quotations

"Say only those things about people that you would want them to hear."

"It is better to light one candle than to curse the darkness."

"O God, grant us the serenity to accept what cannot be changed; the courage to change what can be changed, and the wisdom to know the one from the other." (Reinhold Niebuhr)

"We never really find out what believe in until we begin to instruct our children."

"Some people claim they are troubled by parts of the Bible which they cannot understand. What troubles me is that part of the Bible which I understand only too well...." (Mark Twain)

"In matters of principle stand like a rock; in matters of taste swim with the current." (Thomas Jefferson)

"Your true measure is determined by the way you treat those who can't possibly do you any good."

"In this world we are judged by how many serve us. In the next we will be judged by how many we served."

"If we would use the power that God gives us to see ourselves as others see us, it would from many a blunder and foolish notion free us." (Robert Burns)

"The greatest discovery of any generation is that human beings can alter their lives by altering their attitudes." (Albert Schweitzer)

"I am only one, but I am one. I can't do everything, but I can do something. And what I can do, that ought I to do. And what I ought to do, by the grace of God, I shall do." (Edward Hale)

"If all misfortunes were laid in one common heap whence everyone must take an equal portion, most people would be content to take their own and depart." (Socrates)

Old English Prayer

Take time to work — It is the price of success.

Take time to think — It is the source of power.

Take time to play — It is the secret of perpetual youth.

Take time to read — It is the fountain of wisdom.

Take time to be friendly — It is the road to happiness.

Take time to dream — It is hitching your wagon to a star.

Take time to love and to be loved — It is the privilege of the gods.

Take time to look around — It is too short a day to be selfish.

Take time to laugh — It is music of the soul.

— Anonymous

On This Day

Mend a quarrel. Seek out a forgotten friend.
Write a love letter. Share a treasure.
Encourage a young person. Keep a promise.
Find the time. Count your blessings.
Forego a grudge. Forgive someone.
Listen. Give a soft answer.
Apologize if you were wrong.
Try to understand that certain person.
Examine your demands on someone.
Appreciate. Express your gratitude.
Be kind. Be gentle.
Laugh a little more. Show enthusiasm all day.
Welcome a stranger.
Gladden the heart of a child.
Take pleasure in the beauty and wonder of the earth.
Speak your love. Speak it again. Speak it still again.

— Anonymous

The Optimist's Creed

To be so strong that nothing can disturb your peace of mind.
To talk health, happiness and prosperity to every person you
   meet.
To make all your friends feel that there is something in them.
To look at the sunny side of everything and make your optimism
   come true.
To think only of the best, to work only for the best and to expect
   only the best.
To be just as enthusiastic about the success of others as you are
   about your own.
To forget the mistakes of the past and press on to the greater
   achievements of the future.
To wear a cheerful countenance at all times and give every living

creature you meet a smile.

To give so much time to the improvement of yourself that you have no time to criticize others.

To be too large for worry, too noble for anger, too strong for fear and too happy to permit the presence of trouble.

— Anonymous

A Prayer for Growing Old Gracefully

Lord, Thou knowest better than I myself, that I am growing older and will someday be old. Keep me from the fatal habit of thinking I must say something on every subject and on every occasion. Release me from craving to straighten out everybody's affairs. Make me thoughtful but not moody; helpful but not bossy. With my vast store of wisdom, it seems a pity not to use it all; but Thou knowest, Lord, that I want a few friends at the end. Keep my mind free from the recital of endless details; give me wings to get to the point. Seal my lips on my aches and pains; they are increasing, and love of rehearsing them is becoming sweeter as the years go by. I dare not ask for improved memory, but for a growing humility, and a lessening cocksureness when my memory seems to clash with the memories of others. Teach me the glorious lesson that occasionally I may be mistaken. Keep me reasonably sweet, for a sour old person is one of the crowning works of the devil. Give the ability to see good things in unexpected places and talents in unexpected people, and give, O Lord, the grace to tell them so. Amen.

— Anonymous

Religion

I believe in Christianity; that it is the religion taught to men by God Himself in Person on earth. I also believe the Bible to be a Divine revelation. Christianity is not comparable with any other religion. It is the religion which came from God's own lips, and therefore the only true religion. The incarnation is a fact, and Christianity is based on revealed truth.

There are some books that are absolutely indispensable to the kind of education that we are contemplating, and to the profession that we are now considering; and of all these, the most indispensable, the most useful, the one whose knowledge is most effective, is the Bible.

There is no Book from which more valuable lessons can be learned. I am considering it now as a manual of utility, or professional preparation, and professional use for a journalist.

There is no Book which is more suggestive and more instructive, from which you learn more directly that sublime simplicity which never exaggerates, which recounts the greatest even with solemnity, of course, but without sentimentality or affection, none which you open with such confidence and lay down with such reverence; there is no Book like the Bible.

When you get into a controversy and want exactly the right answer, when you are looking for an expression, what is there that closes a dispute like a verse from the Bible? What is it that sets up the right principle for you, which pleads for a policy, for a cause, so much as the right passage of the Holy Scripture?

— Charles Anderson Dana (1819-1897)

What Teenagers Expect from Parents But often Deny It

To hear the good things along with the bad.

To behave the way you want them to behave.

To build them up along with tearing them down.

To follow through on what you say.

To have as many meals together as possible.

To limit their TV viewing,

To do things as a family.

To expect the best from them.

To insist on responsible behavior.

To abstain from sexual immorality.

To insist on a curfew time.

To forget their mistakes.

To raise them according to biblical principles.

To be a good role model, like admitting mistakes.

To not expect perfection.

To check out their friends — "When you walk with a cripple you learn to limp."

To not avoid the hard issues.

To allow them to make important decisions in preparation for leaving the nest. After all, it's only a few years away!

Why? It shows you care!

Why It Is Good for Us
Not to Have Everything Our Own Way

It's good for you to go through difficult times now and again, and to have your will thwarted; the effect is often to make a man think — make him realize that he is living in exile, and it is no use relying upon any earthly support. It's good for you sometimes to hear men's voices raised against you, and to find that you are making a bad impression, or at least a false impression, on others, even when you are doing your best, and with the best intentions. It often makes for humility; prevents you from having too good an opinion of yourself. It's when we make a bad surface impression, and people are ready to think ill of us, that we learn to fall back upon God's judgments, because he witnesses all of our actions from within.

And that is what we are aiming at; a man ought to rely so firmly on God that he has no need to be always looking about for human support.

A good Christian man can drive profit from the afflictions, the temptations, the unhallowed thoughts which assail him. At such times, he realizes more than ever his need of God; he becomes conscious that no power for good lies in him, apart from divine grace.

— Thomas à Kempis

Wise Sayings

Love your neighbors, but don't pull down your hedges.

A long life may not be good enough, but a good life is long enough.

A good example is the best sermon.

Search others for their virtues, thyself for thy vices.

If you would keep your secret from an enemy, tell it not to a friend.

I have lived, sir, a long time. And the longer I live, the more convincing proofs I see of this truth — that God governs in the affairs of men. And if a sparrow cannot fall on the ground without His notice, is it probable that an empire can rise without His aid?

We have been assured, sir, in the sacred writings that except the Lord build the house, they labor in vain that built it. I firmly believe this; and I also believe that without His concurring aid we shall succeed in this political building no better than the builders of Babel; our projects will be confounded and we ourselves shall become a reproach and a byword down to future ages.

I believe in one God, the Creator of the universe. That He governs it by His providence. That He ought to be worshipped. That the most acceptable service we render Him is doing good to His other children. That the soul of man is immortal, and will be treated with justice in another life respecting its conduct in this.

— Benjamin Franklin

Work

One of the goals of parenting is to make work meaningful to children. It's very important children learn to work as soon as possible. Good work habits will help them with their schoolwork because school is work. Work teaches responsibility, a sense of accomplishment, self-satisfaction, and preparation for life. Parents should:

Assign tasks that are appropriate to age.
Work along with children.
Not expect perfection.
Make work appear pleasant.
Not pay for doing routine chores.
Encourage and praise generously.
Require that children do their best.
Follow through with assigned tasks.

The sooner parents expect responsible behavior from their children, the sooner they will come through.

One Nation Without God

Introduction

We live in a complex and fast-changing world. Many of the issues that surround us are challenging, disturbing, and frightening. Peer pressures, gambling, the feminist movement, marital infidelity, premarital sex, unwed births, absent parents, single-parent homes and step families, more liberal morals, violent crimes, increased lack of respect for authority, and a substantial weakening of the institution of marriage in our courts are just a few of the modern cultural trends that affect all of us.

Although changes occur gradually from one generation to the next, they become more apparent over longer periods of time. Consider the following: smaller families, bigger homes, people living longer, computer technology, modern medicine, more conveniences, two-income families, day-care centers, fast foods, disposable products, home schooling, dress, music, entertainment, increased leisure time. It takes a long period of time to recognize the negative or positive impact each of these changes will have on our society.

The purpose of this section is to first identify the causes of some of these cultural changes. The second is to help people better prepare themselves and their families to face these changes. Finally, I hope the reader will recognize his or her responsibility to play a part, large or small, in restoring the principles that made this nation so great.

I hope, by some of the research and statistics I've included, you'll be able to draw some of your own conclusions to the consequences of these trends and the needed cultural responses.

— Dan Taddeo

A random selection arranged alphabetically follows:

Baby Boom

In 2006, for the first time in America, more than half of babies born to women younger than 30 — 50.4 percent — were born to unwed mothers. That should give Americans pause, because of the poverty and other harmful consequences associated with single parenthood. Some single mothers, especially those closer to thirty, will encounter more hurdles than their married counterparts, but they are more likely to succeed if they've earned a college degree and have a good job and a strong support network. But younger women who are alone and not prepared for motherhood face huge problems with significant implications for their children and the public that must support families that can't support themselves.

Having children without two parents is a recipe for poverty. Young, single mothers face enormous challenges in getting the education needed to launch a career. Many don't graduate from high school. Even more don't go to college, and if they do, they don't graduate. Lifetime earnings potential is severely reduced without a degree.

Many of these struggling single-parent families don't pay taxes; about 40% are below or near the poverty level and need public assistance. Each family headed by a woman who hasn't graduated from high school costs the public about $7,000 a year to support.

Society is not going to return to the 1950s and traditional male and female roles, but it still needs an ethic about the responsibilities of making and raising babies. (*The Plain Dealer* (Cleveland), September 21, 2008)

The negative consequences not noted in this editorial are endless: sexual diseases, regrets, guilt, abortion, child abuse, to mention a few. Unwed mothers can't even begin to imagine what lies ahead. What values will they pass on to their children? God's word does not detail the impact of illicit sex, but it does say that it is wrong.

The Bible

The Bible is a library of sacred writings that reveals God's Word dating back thousands of years before Christ. It was written over a 1,500-year period by forty authors in three different languages on three continents, in ten countries, in 1,551 places, depicting 2,930 characters and without any contradictions.

The Bible contains 66 books divided into two parts: the Old Testament with 39 books (about 593,000 words) beginning with creation and continuing with the history and prophecies of the nation of Israel. The New Testament with 27 books (about 180,000 words) focuses on the birth, life, death, and resurrection of Jesus and the work of his disciples during the first-century AD.

A proper understanding of the Scriptures requires the study of the complete Book. This will reveal its overall theme: God's claim to rule mankind and to make known His loving purpose to everyone.

The Bible is more than a historical document to be preserved. Its language is plain, direct, and meaningful. It touches on geography, history, science, philosophy, ethics — in fact, every area of human thought including marriage, family, and friends. Although God's prophets and followers of Jesus wrote the actual words, God directed their thoughts, making it his infallible and authoritative Word.

The Bible is unquestionably the most important book in history. Two thousand years have passed since its last recorded words. Unlike other books, it has never dwindled into oblivion. Here's what some have said about it:

The Bible is in a class of its own. Year after year, more copies than any other book are printed, circulated, and translated into over 2,000 languages. It speaks to the small child yet challenges the greatest intellects. The New Testament records the events and sayings of Jesus and the work of his apostles. He is by far the most significant and influential person in the Bible and the world.

Changes

As a school counselor, I was constantly searching for answers to such questions as to why certain children felt accepted while others felt rejected; why certain ones had high self-esteem while others felt unworthy; why certain children felt loved while others didn't; why certain ones succeeded while others failed. The conclusion that I came to was that children reared by parents who lived by the Ten Commandments was the single most important factor that accounted for the differences in their behavior.

Typical school related problems at that time were talking, running, gum chewing, tardiness, and uncompleted homework. Today, they include alcohol and drug addition, disobedience, flagrant truancy, student and teacher assaults, pregnancies, abortions, and venereal disease. Back then a school nurse needed permission to give a student an aspirin; now a student can have an abortion without the parent's knowledge.

One major contributor to these negative changes relate to recent Supreme Court decisions:

1962: Banned prayer in America's Public Schools. (Unfortunately, this was at the time when the country needed it most!)

1963: Banned school Bible reading and reciting the Lord's Prayer.

1973: Legalized abortion.

1980: Banned the display of the Ten Commandments in public schools.

1992: Banned prayer at graduations.

Since the early 1960s the liberal judicial activists have made a successful concerted effort to banish God from the public square.

You just cannot get rid of God and expect things to get better. They won't; they'll get worse because people will replace the true God with false ones: greed, wealth, power, fame, self-centeredness, or some other idol. History shows that the loosening of moral bonds is the first stage of disintegration.

Eradication of biblical principles from all public places was never the intention of the country's founders. This would make separation of church and state become all state and no church, thus elevating atheism to the state religion.

Education

During the first two hundred years of America's existence, the education of our children was in the hands of parents or the churches. There was no such thing as public education. During the next one hundred years, state education came into being and education became more and more secular in nature.

One hundred years after that, in the twentieth century, the modern progressive educational movement evolved and spread out across America. A revolution in education was in the making: It would produce an educational system where humans rather than God would be the focus — the birth of humanism.

Sir Julian Huxley, one of this century's leading humanists, said: "I use the word 'humanist' to mean someone who believes — that man is just as much a natural phenomenon as an animal or plant: that his body, mind, and soul were not supernaturally created but are products of evolution; and that he is not under the control or guidance of any supernatural being or beings, but has to rely on himself and his own powers."

The trademarks of humanism, agnosticism, atheism, and secularism are many. There are no eternal standards of truth. All is relative. There are no moral absolutes. There is nothing that is right or wrong. These closed ideologies will always attempt to exclude any mention of biblical principles. They replace God's moral standards with situational ethics. So, instead of relying on God's word, the humanists appoint self and at the center. They then become god — ever changing — and call all the shots.

"The philosophy of the school in one generation will become the philosophy of the government in the next." (Abraham Lincoln)

Family Values

Children's minds at birth are like newly plowed fields. What grows will be determined by the quality of the soil, the kind of seeds planted, and the care given. These factors will determine the quality and quantity of fruit produced. Something is going to grow, if not good seeds then weeds. Once the seeds are planted, the kind of fruit won't change.

God's love binds families together like nothing else. But when families drift away from God's Word, the family unit begins to collapse. Moral deterioration sets in and disrespect for authority takes over. When biblical principles are practiced in the home, children understand that the family unit comes first and they respond accordingly. God's word provides guidance, wisdom, comfort, peace, and the strength needed for parents to remain happily married and successfully raise their children.

"With the family influence gone, what I call vertical transmission of values from one generation to the next is gone, too. All you're left with is horizontal transmission of values through the influence of peers and other contemporary sources of information, such as research studies, news media, and the entertainment-advertising industry." (Robert S. Mendelsohn, M.D.)

The Family

Modern cultural trends continue their devastating effect on the family: More working mothers, half the children raised in broken homes, family time replaced with electronic entertainment and video games. Childcare has shifted from the parents to other agencies causing very limited meaningful conversations between parents and children on a daily basis. After school activities result in many families not eating meals together and when they do, over half of those have the television on during dinner. Television not only isolates the family unit, but also it provides sitcoms that portray parents (especially dads!) as irrelevant and stupid while disobedience and disrespect for parents are considered normal behavior.

More time spent in front of the television, more debt necessitating two working parents, and the societal liberation of the woman from having to raise her own children at home all adds up to less and less time parents spend with children. The result is a generation making important moral decisions apart from the influence of their parents.

Children have less value for their lives and the lives of others today because Mom and Dad value them less. The satisfaction of rearing a loved child has been replaced by the rewards of having a career or building a reputation. Kids are going off the deep end because their parents aren't there to stop them. We are seeing in our children the results of a generation where Mom and Dad are around less and less.

Heredity and Environment

Children respond to their environment based to a great extent on their inherited characteristics. However, they should not be made to feel inferior or cheated because of hereditary differences. They have no control over it. They can't change it. Their worth as a human being should not depend on it.

It's God's plan for them to be different. Therefore, they should not be compared to one another. When parents view their children in this light, they not only prevent them from feeling inferior, but also they actually help them discover God's plan for their lives.

One of the most critical factors in children's lives is their environment. At the moment of conception, environment impacts on children physically, emotionally, and mentally. Since heredity is predetermined, there's little parents can do about it. But they can do a lot about the child's environment and this can make the biggest difference in how a child turns out. It's up to parents to provide a good environment for their children. A healthy environment would include such things as:

Providing safe conditions in which to grow up;
Adapting discipline to the individual child;
Spending as much time as possible with them;
Correcting them in a loving way;
Focusing on their strengths;
Instilling a positive attitude;
"Catching" them doing right;
Helping them acquire a healthy self-image;
Making children feel special;
Supplying healthy physical and spiritual food.

Everything children experience in the environment is recorded in their minds — forever! The more caring the environment, the better children will respond and thrive.

Obedience

Instilling obedience in children is one of the most important and challenging responsibilities of parenting. Parents who really love their children do not overlook or accept excuses for inappropriate behavior. Because children are so different, parents need to learn about their unique traits and discipline them accordingly. Children need to adapt to parents and not the other way around. The family is not a democracy.

Parents need to teach their children right from wrong and hold them to it. They should mean what they say or not say it. Always follow through. Disobedient children feel confused, frustrated, and unloved. They're miserable and make others miserable. Expect children to obey and they will.

It is normal for children to have problems. When they are little, they have little problems that seem big to them. As they get bigger, their problems seem even bigger. Parents need to have frequent conversations about these matters. If they don't, attitudes and values will be formed via outside sources. Getting the whole family together at mealtimes is an ideal time to discuss any family concerns. People are usually in a good mood and they are automatically encouraged to talk and share with one another. This almost guarantees at least one place where they can feel accepted.

Children thrive when parents provide strong leadership in the family. Building family ties and loyalty can be achieved through activities, such as family devotions, church attendance, Bible study, pleasant mealtime conditions, family picnics, vacations, family reunions, keeping family traditions alive, and starting new traditions. These experiences all contribute to enrich and strengthen the family. Entire civilizations rise and fall on the strength of the family.

Parenting

Parents are the first and most important teachers their children will ever have. Informal learning takes place in the home through experience and example. Whatever children learn in the home, right and wrong, tends to remain with them throughout life. They will insist something they learned at home is right even when it's wrong. It is very difficult to switch from one to the other.

Children are more receptive to discipline when they sense that their parents love them; because, subconsciously, they know they care. Children are capable of learning and understanding much more than most parents think. Successful parents answer their children's question with patience and good humor. They will respect and love you for it. It's good to praise them publicly and discipline privately.

Some guiding principles for parenting would include such things as:

Setting reasonable standards of behavior and seeing that they are met.

Providing early opportunities for responsibilities and decision-making appropriate to their age level.

Teaching them that they are no less or no more important than anybody else.

And don't compare them with others, rather have them compete against themselves.

"Let each one examine his own work, then he will have rejoicing in himself alone, without comparing himself to anybody else" (Galatians 6:4).

Parents will influence children more by their actions than what they say. Boys lean more toward imitating their fathers and girls their mothers. This is very healthy when parents are good role models. Parents have to be with their children especially during the preschool years because learning is an ongoing process. In children's eyes their parents are God. So, before they can teach their children about God, they must make sure they are representing Him accurately.

Parents

You shall hold no other group more important than the family and in all thy ways be faithful to it.

You shall teach thy sons and daughters to love, respect, and obey their parents.

You shall be a loving, considerate husband/wife.

You shall not speak in a manner unbecoming a Christian person.

You shall, by example, make Sunday a special day set aside for God and for worship as a family.

You shall provide for thy family spiritually and physically in an adequate manner.

You shall promote and lead family worship in thy home.

You shall be honest in thy dealings.

You shall respect the desires and freedoms of thy family as individuals.

You shall be head of the household, while ruling it with love.

— Anonymous

Prayer's Proper Place

In order to understand the importance of prayer, we must first recognize that peaceful coexistence in a society is a gift from God. It has nothing to do with our ingenuity, planning, wealth, or power but is dependent solely upon the grace of God in response to our steadfast petitions.

That is why the apostle Paul was emphatic that Christians pray continually for the church and governing powers: "I want men everywhere to lift up holy hands in prayer, without anger or disputing" (1 Timothy 2:8).

"The Christian who is still carnal has neither desire nor strength to follow after God. He rests satisfied with the prayer of habit or custom."(Andrew Murray, *The Prayer Life*)

"As the Church, we can no more create a peaceful existence, righteous government or safe living environment than we can cause spiritual growth and revival. When the Church begins to take for granted God's work in a society by relying more on human effort than repentance and prayer, it risks the very thing it is trying so hard to achieve." (Matt Finneran)

Requirements for Living

"What does the Lord require of you? To act justly and to love mercy and to walk humbly with your God" (Micah 6:8).

Act justly — fairness, goodness, honesty. "Blessed are they who maintain justice, who constantly do what is right" (Psalm 106:3).

Love mercy — forgiveness, kindness, thoughtfulness. "Show mercy and compassion to one another" (Zechariah 7:8).

Walk humbly — gentleness, meekness, politeness. "All of you, live in harmony with one another; be sympathetic; live as brothers, be compassionate and humble" (1 Peter 3:8).

God's perfection should be our example and goal. Fortunately, He forgives our imperfections. However, He does expect us to do our best in whatever we are called to do. All those who do receive a grade of A+, because God doesn't grade on the curve!

When Jesus was asked which is the greatest commandment in the law, He replied: "Love the Lord your God with all your heart and with all your soul and with all your mind." This is the first and greatest commandment. And the second is similar to it: "Love your neighbor as yourself" (Matthew 22:36-39).

Restoring the Family

The family is the foundational institution of society. It is the first place where children learn moral values, such as honesty, fairness, and dependability. Children look at life through the lens of the home and see parents for exactly what they are. Since their ability to learn is like radar, they will pick up on whatever their parents stand for. Children can't be fooled for long. Parents have the most influence on children's moral and ethical values, followed by friends, teachers, and clergy.

Remember three things: Children don't expect perfect parents; good intentions count for everything; being honest is critical!

Most of all, the parents' personal lives should serve as a model. This is done best by what parents do rather than by what they say. The power of the example is the most dominant force in child development. Being good role models and surrounding your children with other adults and children that demonstrate equally strong role models are the best ways to guarantee your child will grow up with those same characteristics.

It was said once that the best way for a father to love his children is to love his wife. A strong marriage communicates compassion and caring to the children and provides a secure environment for the children to grow up in. Parents that get along well have gone through the maturing process it takes to have a good relationship with another human being. This naturally carries on over to the raising of the children, who are not only loved more, but are also given a living example of what it means to sacrifice and care for another person.

Right or Wrong

Although there are exceptions, most people agree that a universal standard of morality does exist, which includes virtues, such as fairness, honesty, respect, honor, loyalty, kindness, dependability, and the Golden Rule. Any kind of order is impossible unless all civilized people have some set of nonnegotiable principles that determine their actions.

It is innate for people to appeal to a standard of behavior which they expect others to also follow and understand. "That's not fair," or, "How would you like it if anyone did that to you?" are thought processes that have no racial or cultural boundaries. C. S. Lewis wrote, "We know that men find themselves under a moral law, which they did not make, and cannot quite forget even when they try, and which they know they ought to obey."

Those who believe in the Bible understand that it is God who put a moral law into our minds that we know we ought to obey. Because God created people with a free will, they can choose to do right or wrong. When an individual decides to do wrong, there are consequences to himself or others involved; when a whole society violates this moral code, there is the possible disintegration of that society as a whole.

When it comes to what is really important, we must admit that certain rights and wrongs never change. They are timeless truths that provide guidance when facing tough issues. They worked in the past. They work in the present. They will continue to be true and work in the future.

Society and the Bible

Our Founding Fathers believed in the God of the Bible and established our nation under that God. The inspirational writings and speeches of our national governing officials have been accurately recorded and well documented for all to see, some of which are:

"Whoever is an avowed enemy of God, I scruple not [do not hesitate] to call him an enemy of this country." (John Witherspoon, 1723-1794)

"Whatever may be conceded to the influence of refined education on minds of peculiar structure, reason and experience both forbid us to expect that national morality can prevail in exclusion of religious principle." (George Washington, Farewell Address, 1796)

"No book in the world deserves to be so unceasingly studied, and so profoundly meditated upon as the Bible." (John Quincy Adams, 1812)

The Holy Bible was found to have directly contributed to 34% of all quotes by the Founding Fathers. This was discovered after reviewing 15,000 items from the Founders (including newspaper articles, pamphlets, books, monographs, etc.). The other main sources that the Founders quoted include: Blackstone, 1723-1780; Locke, 1632-1704; Montesquieu, 1689-1755; Pufendorf, 1632-1694. These men took 60% of their quotes directly from the Bible. Direct and indirect quotes combined reveal that 94% of all the quotes of the Founding Fathers are derived from the Bible.

Standing Against the Tide

Abraham Lincoln, sixteenth President of these United States, is everlasting in the memory of this country. For on the battleground of Gettysburg, this is what he said: "The occasion is piled high with difficulty, and we must rise with the occasion. We must disenthrall ourselves and then we shall save our country."

At that time slavery divided and threatened our country. Some 150 years later the unraveling of the family and undermining of our moral foundations has become that threat. What Lincoln said then applies equally today: The occasion "piled high with difficulty" is the eternal struggle between two principles: right and wrong. We must rebuild the foundation of our country by restoring, renewing, and strengthening the moral values upon which it was founded... "and then we shall save our country."

Why have special interest groups and organizations like the ACLU and Americans United for the Separation of Church and State, who represent only a small minority of Americans, been so successful at constantly seeking ways to remove religion from both our private and public lives by subtly twisting the First Amendment? For the answer in part we need to look at our voting record. In the words of Edmund Burke, "The only thing necessary for the triumph of evil is for good men to do nothing."

Over half of all eligible voters in America don't vote for governors, members of Congress, or presidential candidates.

— Matt Finneran

"I am only one, but I am one. I cannot do everything, but I can do something. What I can do, I should do and, with the help of God, I will do!"

— Edward Everett Hale

Scripture Servings for Spiritual Strength

Introduction

There is great value in appreciating what Scripture says about itself. We are told it acts as a lamp of wisdom to guide our every decision and an illumination to the very secrets of our own souls. Those who mediate on it will guard their hearts from sinning and find strength to walk in the ways of God. We are reminded that God Himself watches over every word of Scripture to guarantee its fulfillment and that in these words alone will one discover the way to eternal life.

This section of the book can be used as a unique daily devotional because it contains no commentary or application save the conviction of the Scriptures themselves upon the heart of the reader. You will find plenty to nourish your daily appetite for uplifting promises, godly wisdom, and challenging personal insights that draw you closer to Christ simply by reflecting on Scriptures relating to each topic.

C. S. Lewis once said, "People need more to be reminded than to be instructed."

— Dan Taddeo

A random selection arranged alphabetically follows:

Accountability

When I say to the wicked, "O wicked man you will surely die," and you do not speak out to dissuade him from his way, that wicked man will die for his sin, and I will hold you accountable for his blood (Ezekiel 3:18).

But I tell you that men will have to give account on the day of judgment for every careless word they have spoken. For by your words you will be justified, and by your words you will be condemned (Matthew 12:36-37).

For the Son of Man will come in the glory of His Father with His angels, and then He will reward each according to his works (Matthew 16:27).

For there is nothing covered that will not be revealed nor hidden that will not be known (Luke 12:2).

Whatever the Law says, it speaks to those who are under the Law, that every mouth may be closed and all the world may become accountable to God (Romans 3:19).

So then, each of us will give an account of himself to God (Romans 14:12).

Nothing in all creation is hidden from God's sight. Everything is uncovered and laid bare before the eyes of him to whom we must give account (Hebrews 4:13).

They will give an account to Him who is ready to judge the living and the dead (1 Peter 4:5).

Behavior

Therefore let us stop passing judgment on one another. Instead, make up your mind not to put any stumbling block or obstacle in your brother's way (Romans 14:13).

We who are strong ought to bear with the failings of the weak and not to please ourselves (Romans 15:1).

So whether you eat or drink or whatever you do, do it all for the glory of God (1 Corinthians 10:31).

Bear one another's burdens, and so fulfill the law of Christ (Galatians 6:2).

Do not be deceived: God cannot be mocked. A man reaps what he sows (Galatians 6:7).

And let us not grow weary while doing good, for in due season we shall reap if we do not lose heart (Galatians 6:9).

Do nothing out of selfish ambition or vain conceit, but in humility consider others better than yourselves (Philippians 2:3).

Your attitude should be the same as that of Christ Jesus (Philippians 2:5).

Do your best to present yourself to God as one approved, a workman who does not need to be ashamed and who correctly handles the word of truth (2 Timothy 2:15).

Charity

Blessed is he who has regard for the weak; the Lord delivers him in times of trouble (Psalm 41:1).

A generous man will prosper; he who refreshes others will himself be refreshed (Proverbs 11:25).

He who is kind to the poor lends to the Lord, and He will reward him for what he has done (Proverbs 19:17).

And if you spend yourselves in behalf of the hungry and satisfy the needs of the oppressed, then your light will rise in the darkness, and your night will become like the noonday (Isaiah 58:10).

[Jesus said,] "The King will reply, 'I tell you the truth, whatever you did for one of the least of these brothers of mine, you did for Me" (Matthew 25:40).

Give, and it will be given to you. A good measure, pressed down, shaken together and running over, will be poured into your lap. For with the measure you use, it will be measured to you (Luke 6:38).

So let each one give as he purposes in his heart, not grudgingly or of necessity; for God loves a cheerful giver (2 Corinthians 9:7).

Therefore, as we have opportunity, let us do good to all, especially to those who are of the household of faith (Galatians 6:10).

Conduct

Do not let this Book of the Law depart from your mouth; meditate on it day and night, so that you may be careful to do everything written in it. Then you will be prosperous and successful (Joshua 1:8).

Do not withhold good from those to whom it is due when it is in the power of your hand to do so (Proverbs 3:26-27).

He who walks with integrity walks securely, But he who perverts his ways will become known (Proverbs 10:9).

Commit to the Lord whatever you do, and your plans will succeed (Proverbs 16:3).

Even a child is known by his deeds, whether what he does is pure and right (Proverbs 20:11).

I the Lord search the heart and examine the mind, to reward a man according to his conduct, according to what his deeds deserve (Jeremiah 17:10).

I dispersed them among the nations, and they were scattered through the countries; I judged them according to their conduct and their actions (Ezekiel 36:19).

Do you not know that those who run in a race all run, but one receives the prize? Run in such a way that you may obtain it (1 Corinthians 9:24).

Discernment

So give Your servant a discerning heart to govern your people and to distinguish between right and wrong. For who is able to govern this great people of Yours? (1 Kings 3:9).

I am Your servant; give me discernment that I may understand Your statutes (Psalm 119:125).

O Lord, You have searched me and You know me. You discern my going out and my lying down; You are familiar with all my ways. You know when I sit and when I rise; You perceive my thoughts from afar. Before a word is on my tongue You know it completely, O Lord (Psalm 139:1-3).

A rebuke impresses a man of discernment more than a hundred lashes a fool (Proverbs 17:10).

Even a fool is thought wise if he keeps silent, and discerning if he holds his tongue (Proverbs 17:28).

Whoever keeps the law is a discerning son, but a companion of gluttons shames his father (Proverbs 28:7).

The man without the Spirit does not accept the things that come from the Spirit of God, for they are foolishness to him, and he cannot understand them, because they are spiritually discerned (1 Corinthians 2:14).

For he who eats and drinks in an unworthy manner eats and drinks judgment to himself, not discerning the Lord's body (1 Corinthians 11:29).

Endurance

May His name endure forever; may it continue as long as the sun. All nations will be blessed through Him, and they will call Him blessed (Psalm 72:17).

Fear not, for I am with you. Be not dismayed, for I am your God. I will strengthen you. Yes, I will help you. I will uphold you with My righteous right hand (Isaiah 41:10).

"For I know the plans I have for you," declares the Lord, "plans to prosper you and not to harm you, plans to give you hope and a future" (Jeremiah 29:11).

Can your heart endure, or can your hands remain strong, in the days when I shall deal with you? I, the Lord, have spoken, and will do it (Ezekiel 22:14).

And you will be hated by all for My name's sake. But he who endures to the end will be saved (Matthew 10:22).

And they have no root in themselves, and so endure only for a time. Afterward, when tribulation or persecution arises for the word's sake, immediately they stumble (Mark 4:17).

[Love] bears all things, believes all things, hopes all things, endures all things (1 Corinthians 13:7).

Endure hardship as a discipline; God is treating you as sons. For what son is not disciplined by his father? (Hebrews 12:7).

Favoritism

Do not pervert justice; do not show partiality to the poor or favoritism to the great, but judge your neighbor fairly (Leviticus 19:15).

I will show partiality to no one, nor will I flatter any man (Job 32:21).

Then Peter began to speak: "I now realize how true it is that God does not show favoritism" (Acts 10:34).

And masters, treat your slaves in the same way. Do not threaten them, since you know that he who is both their Master and yours is in heaven, and there is no favoritism with him (Ephesians 6:9).

Anyone who does wrong will be repaid for this wrong, and there is no favoritism (Colossians 3:25).

I charge you, in the sight of God and Christ Jesus and the elect angels, to keep these instructions without partiality, and to do nothing out of favoritism (1 Timothy 5:21).

My brothers, as believers in our glorious Lord Jesus Christ, don't show favoritism (James 2:1).

If you really keep the royal law found in Scripture, "Love your neighbor as yourself," you are doing right. But if you show favoritism, you sin and are convicted by the law as lawbreakers (James 2:8-9).

Forgiveness

The Lord is slow to anger, abounding in love and forgiving sin and rebellion. Yet He does not leave the guilty unpunished; He punishes the children for the sin of the fathers to the third and fourth generation (Numbers 14:18).

And forgive us our debts, as we forgive our debtors (Matthew 6:12).

For if you forgive men their trespasses, your heavenly Father will also forgive you (Matthew 6:14).

But if you do not forgive men their trespasses, neither will your Father forgive your trespasses (Matthew 6:15).

And repentance and forgiveness of sins will be preached in His name to all nations, beginning at Jerusalem (Luke 24:47).

All the prophets testify about Him that everyone who believes in Him receives forgiveness of sins through His name (Acts 10:43).

In Him we have redemption through His blood, the forgiveness of sins, according to the riches of His grace (Ephesians 1:7).

If we confess our sins, He is faithful and just to forgive us our sins and to cleanse us from all unrighteousness (1 John 1:9).

Godliness

But You are the same, and Your years will have no end (Psalm 102:27).

O Lord, You have searched me and known me. You know my sitting down and my rising up; You understand my thought afar off. You comprehend my path and my lying down, and are acquainted with all my ways. Before a word is on my tongue you know it completely, O Lord (Psalm 139:1-4).

Call to Me and I will answer you and tell you great and unsearchable things you do not know (Jeremiah 33:3).

No one has ever seen God, but God the One and Only, who is at the Father's side, has made him known (John 1:18).

For God so loved the world that He gave His only begotten Son, that whoever believes in Him should not perish but have everlasting life (John 3:16).

God is Spirit, and those who worship Him must worship in spirit and truth (John 4:24).

But Peter and the other apostles answered and said: "We ought to obey God rather than men" (Acts 5:29).

Every good and perfect gift is from above, coming down from the Father of the heavenly lights, who does not change like shifting shadows (James 1:17).

Grace

For the law was given through Moses, but grace and truth came through Jesus Christ (John 1:17).

Moreover the law entered that the offense might abound. But where sin abounded, grace abounded much more (Romans 5:20).

And God is able to make all grace abound to you, so that in all things at all times, having all that you need, you will abound in every good work (2 Corinthians 9:8).

And He said to me, "My grace is sufficient for you, for My strength is made perfect in weakness." Therefore most gladly I will rather boast in my infirmities, that the power of Christ may rest upon me (2 Corinthians 12:9).

In Him we have redemption through his blood, the forgiveness of sins, in accordance with the riches of God's grace (Ephesians 1:7).

For it is by grace you have been saved, through faith — and this not from yourselves, it is the gift of God — not by works, so that no one can boast (Ephesians 2:8-9).

Let us then approach the throne of grace with confidence, so that we may receive mercy and find grace to help us in our time of need (Hebrews 4:16).

And the grace of our Lord was exceedingly abundant, with faith and love which are in Christ Jesus (1 Timothy 1:14).

Heaven

Behold, I will create new heavens and a new earth. The former things will not be remembered, nor will they come to mind (Isaiah 65:17).

Enter by the narrow gate; for wide is the gate and broad is the way that leads to destruction, and there are many who go in by it (Matthew 7:13).

Because narrow is the gate and difficult is the way which leads to life, and there are few who find it (Matthew 7:14).

Do not be afraid of those who kill the body but cannot kill the soul. Rather, be afraid of the One who can destroy both soul and body in hell (Matthew 10:28).

For God so loved the world that He gave His one and only Son, that whoever believes in Him shall not perish but have eternal life (John 3:16).

That if you confess with your mouth, "Jesus is Lord," and believe in your heart that God raised Him from the dead, you will be saved (Romans 10:9).

But our citizenship is in heaven. And we eagerly await a Savior from there, the Lord Jesus Christ (Philippians 3:20).

[Christ], by the power that enables Him to bring everything under His control, will transform our lowly bodies so that they will be like his glorious body (Philippians 3:21).

Hell

If your right eye causes you to sin, gouge it out and throw it away. It is better for you to lose one part of your body than for your whole body to be thrown into hell (Matthew 5:29).

Enter by the narrow gate; for wide is the gate and broad is the way that leads to destruction, and there are many who go in by it. Because narrow is the gate and difficult is the way which leads to life, and there are few who find it (Matthew 7:13-14).

And do not fear those who kill the body but cannot kill the soul. But rather fear Him who is able to destroy both soul and body in hell (Matthew 10:28).

The Son of Man will send out His angels, and they will weed out of His kingdom everything that causes sin and all who do evil. They will throw them into the fiery furnace, where there will be weeping and gnashing of teeth (Matthew 13:41-42).

Do not marvel at this; for the hour is coming in which all who are in the graves will hear His voice and come forth — those who have done good, to the resurrection of life, and those who have done evil, to the resurrection of condemnation (John 5:28-29).

And anyone not found written in the Book of Life was cast into the lake of fire (Revelation 20:15).

Light

There are those who rebel against the light; they do not know its ways nor abide in its paths (Job 24:13).

God is the Lord, and he has given us light (Psalm 118:27).

The people who walked in darkness have seen a great light; those who dwelt in the land of the shadow of death, upon them a light has shined (Isaiah 9:2).

Let your light so shine before men, that they may see your good works and glorify your Father in heaven (Matthew 5:16).

The eye is the lamp of the body. If your eyes are good, your whole body will be full of light. But if your eyes are bad, your whole body will be full of darkness. If then the light within you is darkness, how great is that darkness! (Matthew 6:22-23).

Then Jesus spoke to them again, saying, "I am the light of the world. He who follows Me shall not walk in darkness, but have the light of life" (John 8:12).

But you are a chosen generation, a royal priesthood, a holy nation, His own special people, that you may proclaim the praises of Him who called you out of darkness into His marvelous light (1 Peter 2:9).

There shall be no night there: They need no lamp nor light of the sun, for the Lord God gives them light. And they shall reign forever and ever (Revelation 22:5).

Lying

You shall not give false testimony against your neighbor (Exodus 20:16).

Truthful lips endure forever, but a lying tongue lasts only a moment (Proverbs 12:19).

The Lord detests lying lips, but He delights in men who are truthful (Proverbs 12:22).

A false witness will not go unpunished, and he who speaks lies will not escape (Proverbs 19:5).

What is desired in a man is kindness, and a poor man is better than a liar (Proverbs 19:22).

Therefore, putting away lying, "Let each one of you speak truth with his neighbor," for we are members of one another (Ephesians 4:25).

Do not lie to each other, since you have taken off your old self with its practices (Colossians 3:9).

If we claim to have fellowship with Him yet walk in the darkness, we lie and do not live by the truth (1 John 1:6).

If anyone says, "I love God," yet hates his brother, he is a liar. For anyone who does not love his brother, whom he has seen, cannot love God, whom he has not seen (1 John 4:20).

Motives

The Lord does not look at the things man looks at. Man looks at the outward appearance, but the Lord looks at the heart (1 Samuel 16:7).

The Lord searches every heart and understands every motive behind the thoughts. If you seek Him, He will be found by you; but if you forsake Him, He will reject you forever (1 Chronicles 28:9).

For a man's ways are in full view of the Lord, and He examines all his paths (Proverbs 5:21).

All a man's ways seem innocent to him, but motives are weighed by the Lord (Proverbs 16:2).

Therefore judge nothing before the appointed time; wait till the Lord comes. He will bring to light what is hidden in darkness and will expose the motives of men's hearts. At that time each will receive his praise from God (1 Corinthians 4:5).

Let nothing be done through selfish ambition or conceit, but in lowliness of mind let each esteem others better than himself (Philippians 2:3).

Let each of you look out not only for his interests, but also for the interests of others (Philippians 2:4).

When you ask, you do not receive, because you ask with wrong motives, that you may spend what you get on your pleasures (James 4:3).

Peer Pressure

Blessed is the man who walks not in the counsel of the ungodly, nor stands in the path of sinners, nor sits in the seat of the scornful (Psalm 1:1).

My son, if sinners entice you, do not give in to them (Proverbs 1:10).

Do not be envious of evil men, nor desire to be with them (Proverbs 24:1).

Enter through the narrow gate. For wide is the gate and broad is the road that leads to destruction, and many enter through it. Because narrow is the gate and difficult is the way which leads to life, and there are few who find it (Matthew 7:13-14).

Watch out for false prophets. They come to you in sheep's clothing, but inwardly they are ferocious wolves (Matthew 7:15).

Do not be misled: "Bad company corrupts good character" (1 Corinthians 15:33).

Your faith should not be in the wisdom of men but in the power of God (Galatians 1:10).

See to it that no one takes you captive through hollow and deceptive philosophy, which depends on human tradition and the basic principles of this world rather than on Christ (Colossians 2:8).

Prayer

Send forth your light and your truth, let them guide me; let them guide me; let them bring me to your holy mountain, to the place where you dwell (Psalm 43:3).

Create in me a clean heart, O God, and renew a steadfast spirit within me. Do not cast me away from Your presence, and do not take Your Holy Spirit from me. Restore to me the joy of Your salvation, and uphold me by Your generous Spirit (Psalm 51:10-12).

Praise be to God, Who has not rejected by prayer or withheld His love from me! (Psalm 66:20).

Watch and pray, lest you enter into temptation. The spirit indeed is willing, but the flesh is weak (Mark 14:38).

One day Jesus was praying in a certain place. When He finished, one of His disciples said to him, "Lord, teach us to pray, just as John taught his disciples" (Luke 11:1).

For this reason I kneel before the Father, from Whom His whole family in heaven and on earth derives its name. I pray that out of His glorious riches He may strengthen you with power through the Spirit in your inner being so that Christ may dwell in your hearts through faith (Ephesians 3:14-17).

Do not be anxious about anything, but in everything, by prayer and petition, with thanksgiving, present your requests to God (Philippians 4:6).

Quarreling

Pride only breeds quarrels, but wisdom is found in those who take advice (Proverbs 13:10).

A hot-tempered man stirs up dissension, but a patient man calms a quarrel (Proverbs 15:18).

Starting a quarrel is like breaching a dam; so drop the matter before a dispute breaks out (Proverbs 17:14).

It is to a man's honor to avoid strife, but every fool is quick to quarrel (Proverbs 20:3).

He who passes by and meddles in a quarrel not his own is like one who takes a dog by the ears (Proverbs 26:17).

Without wood a fire goes out; without gossip a quarrel dies down (Proverbs 26:20).

As charcoal to embers and as wood to fire, so is a quarrelsome man for kindling strife (Proverbs 26:21).

I appeal to you, brethren, in the name of our Lord Jesus Christ, that all of you agree with one another so that there may be no divisions among you (1 Corinthians 1:10).

Don't have anything to do with foolish and stupid arguments, because you know they produce quarrels (2 Timothy 2:23).

And the Lord's servant must not quarrel; instead, he must be kind to everyone, able to teach, not resentful (2 Timothy 2:24).

Salvation

Whoever believes and is baptized will be saved, but whoever does not believe will be condemned (Mark 16:16).

And it shall come to pass that whoever calls on the name of the Lord shall be saved (Acts 2:21).

So they said, "Believe on the Lord Jesus Christ, and you will be saved, you and your household" (Acts 16:31).

That if you confess with your mouth, "Jesus is Lord," and believe in your heart that God raised Him from the dead, you will be saved (Romans 10:9).

For whoever calls on the name of the Lord shall be saved (Romans 10:13).

For the message of the cross is foolishness to those who are perishing, but to us who are being saved it is the power of God (1 Corinthians 1:18).

For it is by grace you have been saved, through faith — and this not from yourselves, it is the gift of God — not by works, so that no one can boast (Ephesians 2:8).

[God] wants all men to be saved and to come to a knowledge of the truth (1 Timothy 2:4).

He saved us, not because of righteous things we had done, but because of His mercy. He saved us through the washing of rebirth and renewal by the Holy Spirit (Titus 3:5).

Sowing/Reaping

As I have observed, those who plow evil and those who sow trouble reap it (Job 4:8).

The wicked man earns deceptive wages, but he who sows righteousness reaps a sure reward (Proverbs 11:18).

Sow for yourselves, reap the fruit of unfailing love, and break up your unplowed ground; for it is time to seek the Lord, until He comes and showers righteousness on you (Hosea 10:12).

Even now the reaper draws his wages, even now he harvests the crop for eternal life, so that the sower and the reaper may be glad together. Thus the saying, "One sows and another reaps" is true (John 4:36-37).

I sent you to reap what you have not worked for. Others have done the hard work, and you have reaped the benefits of their labor (John 4:38).

Remember this: Whoever sows sparingly will also reap sparingly, and whoever sows generously will also reap generously (2 Corinthians 9:6).

And God is able to make all grace abound to you, so that in all things at all times, having all that you need, you will abound in every good work (2 Corinthians 9:8).

Peacemakers who sow in peace raise a harvest of righteousness (James 3:18).

Success

Do not let this Book of the Law depart from your mouth; meditate on it day and night, so that you may be careful to do everything written in it. Then you will be prosperous and successful (Joshua 1:8).

Then you will have success if you are careful to observe the decrees and laws that the Lord gave Moses for Israel. Be strong and courageous. Do not be afraid or discouraged (1 Chronicles 22:13).

He sought God during the days of Zechariah, who instructed him in the fear of God. As long as he sought the Lord, God gave him success (2 Chronicles 26:5).

May He give you the desire of your heart and make all your plans succeed (Psalm 20:4).

Trust in the Lord with all your heart, and lean not on your own understanding. In all your ways acknowledge Him, and He shall direct your paths (Proverbs 3:5-6).

Commit to the Lord whatever you do, and your plans will succeed (Proverbs 16:3).

Whoever gives heed to instruction prospers, and blessed is he who trusts in the Lord (Proverbs 16:20).

There is no wisdom, no insight, no plan that can succeed against the Lord (Proverbs 21:30).

Tongue

The mouth of the righteous man utters wisdom, and his tongue speaks what is just (Psalm 37:30).

Reckless words pierce like a sword, but the tongue of the wise brings healing (Proverbs 12:18).

The tongue that brings healing is a tree of life, but a deceitful tongue crushes the spirit (Proverbs 15:4).

The tongue has the power of life and death, and those who love it will eat its fruit (Proverbs 18:21).

"No weapon forged against you will prevail, and you will refute every tongue that accuses you. This is the heritage of the servants of the Lord, and this is their vindication from me," declares the Lord (Isaiah 54:17).

Even so the tongue is a little member and boasts great things. See how great a forest a little fire kindles! (James 3:5).

But no man can tame the tongue. It is an unruly evil, full of deadly poison (James 3:8).

With the tongue we praise our Lord and Father, and with it we curse men, who have been made in God's likeness. Out of the same mouth come praise and cursing. My brothers, this should not be (James 3:9-10).

Dear children, let us not love with words or tongue but with actions and in truth (1 John 3:18).

Unity

How good and pleasant it is when brothers live together in unity! (Psalm 133:1).

[Jesus prayed,] "I have given them the glory that You gave Me, that they may be one as We are one in them and You in Me. May they be brought to complete unity to let the world know that You sent Me and have loved them even as You have loved Me" (John 17:22-23).

May the God who gives endurance and encouragement give you a spirit of unity among yourselves as you follow Jesus Christ (Romans 15:5).

Be completely humble and gentle; be patient, bearing with one another in love (Ephesians 4:2).

Make every effort to keep the unity of the Spirit through the bond of peace (Ephesians 4:3).

Be kind and compassionate to one another, forgiving each other just as in Christ God forgave you (Ephesians 4:32).

If you have any encouragement from being united with Christ, if any comfort from His love, if any fellowship with the Spirit, if any tenderness and compassion, then make my joy complete by being like-minded, having the same love, being one in spirit and purpose (Philippians 2:1-2).

And over all these virtues put on love, which binds them all together in perfect unity (Colossians 3:14).

Vital Signs

Even a child is known by his actions, by whether his conduct is pure and right (Proverbs 20:11).

But those who hope in the Lord will renew their strength. They will soar on wings like eagles; they will run and not grow weary, they will walk and not faint (Isaiah 40:31).

He has showed you, O man, what is good. And what does the Lord require of you? To act justly and to love mercy and to walk humbly with your God (Micah 6:8).

In the same way, let your light shine before men, that they may see your good deeds and praise your Father in heaven (Matthew 5:16).

But seek first His kingdom and His righteousness, and all these things will be given to you as well (Matthew 6:33).

Do to others as you would have them do to you (Luke 6:31).

You who are trying to be justified by law have been alienated from Christ; you have fallen from grace (Galatians 5:4).

The entire law is summed up in a single command: "Love your neighbor as yourself" (Galatians 5:14).

Those who belong to Christ Jesus have crucified the sinful nature with its passions and desires. Since we live by the Spirit, let us keep in step by the Spirit (Galatians 5:24-25).

Notable Quotables

Introduction

You are holding a selection of the most remarkable assortment of quotations found in one volume — a collection of quotes relevant to every generation and every culture. There is something here for everyone, and the topics are myriad — from birth to death and everything in between.

The material was selected from hundreds of thousands of quotations and proverbs that have come down to us since the dawn of history, and the main criteria for each selection was its ability to inspire, instruct, and challenge people to rise to greater heights.

Truth is truth, no matter where it is found. What you find here is not new revelation, but simply unique ways of expressing ancient wisdom. And as Henry Ward Beecher said, "Wise sayings are lamps that light our way, from the darkness to the light of day."

Compiling those "notable quotables" was one of the most gratifying and rewarding experiences in my life. It became a serendipitous adventure filled with unintentional discoveries that proved to be positive, uplifting and edifying.

— Dan Taddeo

A random selection arranged alphabetically follows:

Action

A thousand words will not leave so deep an impression as one deed. (Henrik Ibsen)

And thou wilt give thyself relief, if thou doest every act of thy life as if it were the last. (Marcus Aurelius)

Do not let what you cannot do interfere with what you can do. (John Wooden)

Do the best you can with what you've got, where you are. (Marchant)

Even a child is known by his actions, by whether his conduct is pure and right. (Proverbs 20:11)

Footprints on the sands of time are not made by sitting down. (Unknown)

I am only one, but I am one. I cannot do everything, but I can do something…. What I can do, I should do. And what I should do, by the grace of God, I will do! (Edward Everett Hale)

If there is no wind, row. (Unknown)

If you're going to do anything, you do it well or don't do it at all. (Hortense Neahr Bloomer)

It is better to light one candle than to curse the darkness. (Unknown)

Each of you should look not only to your own interests, but also to the interests of others. (Philippians 2:4)

Love all, trust a few. Do wrong to none. (William Shakespeare)

Our main business is not to see what lies dimly at a distance, but to do what lies clearly at hand. (Thomas Carlyle)

The smallest good deed is better than the greatest intention. (Unknown)

To do nothing is in every man's power. (Samuel Johnson)

We cannot direct the wind, but we can adjust the sails. (Unknown)

We know what a person thinks not when he tells us what he thinks, but by his actions. (Isaac Bashevis Singer)

Attitude

Attitudes are more important than facts. (Karl Menninger)

If life gives you lemons, make lemonade. (Dale Carnegie)

The remarkable thing is we have a choice every day regarding the attitude we will embrace for that day. We cannot change our past.... We cannot change the fact that people will act in a certain way. We cannot change the inevitable. The only thing we can do is play on the one string we have, and that is our attitude. (Charles Swindoll)

There is little difference in people, but that little difference makes a big difference. The little difference is attitude. The big difference is whether it is positive or negative. (W. Clement Stone)

When our attitude is right, our abilities reach a maximum of effectiveness and good results inevitably follow. (Erwin Schell)

Nothing can stop the man with the right mental attitude from achieving his goal; nothing on earth can help the man with the wrong mental attitude. (Thomas Jefferson)

The greatest discovery of any generation is that human beings can alter their lives by altering their attitudes. (Albert Schweitzer)

When you pray for anyone you tend to modify your personal attitude toward him. You lift the relationship thereby to a higher level. The best in the other person begins to flow toward you as your best flows toward him. In the meeting of the best in each, a higher unity of understanding is established. (Norman Vincent Peale)

Behavior

Anyone can carry his burden, however hard, until nightfall. Anyone can do his work, however hard, for one day. Anyone can live sweetly, patiently, lovingly, purely 'til the sun goes down. And this is all life really means. (Robert Louis Stevenson)

Certain behaviors, due to nature or nurture, are fixed early in childhood and, like a leopard's spots, remain unchanged throughout life. (Charles Panati)

It is easier to give a cup of rice to relieve hunger than to relieve the loneliness and pain of someone unloved in our own home. (Mother Teresa)

Let us remember that our behavior and our upright life will give us respect, dignity, and reverence. (Sami Dagher)

On Judgment Day, God will not ask to what sect you belonged, but what manner of life you led. (I. M. Kagan)

Reprove a friend in secret, but praise him before others. (Leonardo da Vinci)

The impossible is often the untried. (Jim Goodwin)

We have all failed to practice ourselves the kind of behavior we expect from other people. (C. S. Lewis)

We who are strong ought to bear with the failings of the weak and not to please ourselves. (Romans 15:1)

Children

It's better to make a child stretch to reach your high opinion than stoop to match your disrespect. (James Dobson)

Train a child in the way he should go; and when he is old he will not turn from it. (Proverbs 22:6)

All children wear the sign: "I want to be important now." Many of our juvenile delinquency problems arise because nobody read the sign. (Dan Pursuit)

You know children are growing up when they start asking questions that have answers. (John J. Plomp)

You can do anything with children if you only play with them. (Otto von Bismarck)

In bringing up children, spend on them half as much money and twice as much time. (Dr. Laurence J. Peters)

Children should be led into the right path, not by severity, but by persuasion. (Terence)

Children cannot be made good by making them happy, but they can be made happy by making them good. (E. J. Kiefer)

Children have never been very good at listening to their elders, but they have never failed to imitate them. (James Baldwin)

Children need love, especially when they do not deserve it. (Harold S. Hulbert)

There are only two things a child will share willingly — communicable diseases and his mother's age. (Dr. Benjamin Spock)

Teach your [children] how to forgive, make your homes places of love and forgiveness; make your streets and neighborhoods centers of peace and reconciliation. (Pope John Paul II)

Debt

Debt is the slavery of the free. (Publius Syrus)

The rich rule over the poor, and the borrower is servant to the lender. (Proverbs 22:7)

I'm living so far beyond my income that we may almost be said to be living apart. (E. E. Cummings)

Let no debt remain outstanding, except the continuing debt to love one another, for he who loves his fellowman has fulfilled the law. (Romans 13:8)

Part of our problem with debt is that we have confused needs with wants. Yesterday's luxuries are today's necessities. (Billy Graham)

The second vice is lying, the first is running into debt. (Benjamin Franklin)

Think what you do when you run into debt. (Benjamin Franklin)

Will not your debtors suddenly arise? Will they not wake up and make you tremble? Then you will become their victim. (Habakkuk 2:7)

It is hard to pay for bread that has been eaten. (Danish Proverb)

People spend up to a third more when paying with credit instead of cash. (Joan W. Lawrence, Ohio Department of Aging Director)

The borrower is servant to the lender. (Proverbs 22:7)

Eternity

As it was in the beginning, is now, and ever shall be: world without end. (The Book of Common Prayer)

Christians can rejoice in tribulation because they have eternity's values in view. When the pressures are on, they look beyond their present predicament to the glories of heaven. The thoughts of the future life with its prerogatives and joys help to make the trials of the present seem light and transient. (Billy Graham)

Eternity is not something that begins after you are dead. It is going on all the time. We are in it now. (Charlotte Perkins Gilman)

He is no fool who gives what he cannot keep to gain what he cannot lose. (James Elliot, missionary)

One hour of eternity, one moment with the Lord, will make us utterly forget a lifetime of desolations. (Horatius Bonar)

Only what we have wrought into our character during life can we take away with us. (Alexander von Humboldt)

That day, which you fear as being the end of all things, is the birthday of your eternity. (Seneca, 4 BC-65 AD)

The eternal life is not the future life; it is life in harmony with the true order of things — life in God. (Henri Frederic Amiel)

When we become so preoccupied with this life and lose the value of eternity, then we lose this life as well. (C. S. Lewis)

Faith

And without faith it is impossible to please God, because anyone who comes to him must believe that he exists and that he rewards those who earnestly seek him. (Hebrews 11:6)

The Founding Fathers believed that faith in God was the key to our being a good people and America's becoming a great nation. (Ronald Reagan)

We cannot live on probabilities. The faith in which we can live bravely and die in peace must be a certainty, so far as it professes to be a faith at all, or it is nothing. (James A. Froude)

Without faith man becomes sterile, hopeless, and afraid to the very core of his being. (Erich Fromm)

Understanding is the reward of faith. Therefore, seek not to understand that thou mayest believe, but believe that thou mayest understand. (St. Augustine)

We live by faith, not by sight. (2 Corinthians 5:7)

God our Father has made all things depend on faith so that whoever has faith will have everything, and whoever does not have faith will have nothing. (Martin Luther)

Christ has told us "according to your faith, be it unto you." What a wonderful promise in those words. (Norman Vincent Peale)

In the same way, faith by itself, if it is not accompanied by action, is dead. (James 2:17)

For the Lord is good and his love endures forever; his faithfulness continues through all generations. (Psalm 100:5)

God didn't ask me to be successful; He asked me to be faithful. (Mother Teresa)

The presence of faith is no guarantee of deliverance from times of distress and vicissitude, but there can be a certainty that nothing will be encountered that is overwhelming. (William Barr Oglesby Jr.)

Failure

A failure is a man who has blundered but is not able to cash in on the experience. (Elbert Hubbard)

A man can fail many times, but he isn't a failure until he begins to blame somebody else. (John Burroughs)

Fall seven times, stand up eight. (Unknown)

Good people are good because they've come to wisdom through failure. We get very little wisdom from success, you know. (William Saroyan)

I cannot give you the formula for success, but I can give you the formula for failure which is: Try to please everybody. (Herbert Bayard Swope)

I have not failed. I've just found ten thousand ways that won't work. (Thomas Edison)

I never encountered it. All I ever met were temporary setbacks. (Dottie Walters)

Many of life's failures are people who did not realize how close they were to success when they gave up. (Thomas Edison)

Nobody is a total failure if he dares to try to do something worthwhile. (Robert Schuller)

The great question is not whether you have failed, but whether you are content with failure. (Dr. Laurence J. Peter)

There is not failure except in no longer trying. (Elbert Hubbard)

Family

The most meaningful activities in the family are often those simple interactions that build lasting connections between generations. (Dr. James Dobson)

A society without a strong commitment to family and faithful fatherhood will fail to be virtuous at all and will, therefore, sow the seeds of its own destruction. (D. James Kennedy)

Ask yourself every day, "What can I do today to make my wife and family happy?" (David Joseph Schwartz)

All happy families resemble one another; every unhappy family is unhappy in its own way. (Leo Tolstoy)

Everyone who quotes proverbs will quote this proverb about you: Like mother, like daughter. (Ezekiel 16:44)

Fate chooses your relations, you choose your friends. (Jacques Delille)

He who brings trouble on his family will inherit only wind. (Proverbs 11:29)

If a man wants to find God everywhere he must find God somewhere. Particularly in his own family. (Hubert van Zeller)

Perhaps the greatest social service that can be rendered by anybody to the country and to mankind is to bring up a family. (George Bernard Shaw)

The family is the nucleus of civilization. (Will and Ariel Durant)

The family that prays together, stays together is much more than a cliché! And when the family adds the dimension of praying together in church, the truth becomes even stronger. (Zig Ziglar)

The most important thing a father can do for his children is to love their mother. (Theodore Hesburgh)

Forgiveness

One of the most lasting pleasures you can experience is the feeling that comes over you when you genuinely forgive an enemy — whether he knows about it or not. (A. Battista)

Be kind and compassionate to one another, forgiving each other, just as in Christ God forgave you. (Ephesians 4:32)

Forgiveness is not an occasional act: It is an attitude. (Martin Luther King, Jr.)

Forgiveness is perfect when the sin is not remembered. (Unknown)

He who has not forgiven an enemy has never yet tasted one of the most sublime enjoyments of life. (Johann Kaspar Lavater)

I think that if God forgives us we must forgive ourselves. (C. S. Lewis)

The weak can never forgive. Forgiveness is the attribute of the strong. (Mahatma Gandhi)

To err is human, to forgive divine. (Alexander Pope)

We pardon in the degree that we love. (Francois de la Rochefoucauld)

When you forgive, you in no way change the past — but you sure do change the future. (Bernard Meltzer)

Without forgiveness life is governed by... an endless cycle of resentment and retaliation. (Roberto Assagioli)

Friendship

The best thing to do behind a friend's back is pat it. (Ruth Brillhart)

A friend is what the heart needs all the time. (Henry van Dyke)

Be a friend to thyself, and others will be so too. (Thomas Fuller)

He will never have true friends who is afraid of making enemies. (William Hazlitt)

Friendship is born at that moment one person says to another: "What? You, too? I thought I was the only one." (C. S. Lewis)

Friendship is one soul living in two bodies. (Aristotle)

Friendship is really a matter of time... the time that you take when you care. (Amanda Bradley)

Treat a friend as a person who may someday become your enemy; an enemy as a person who may someday become your friend. (George Bernard Shaw)

Two are better than one, because they have a good return for their work: If one falls down, his friend can help him up. (Ecclesiastes 4:9)

Wishing to be friends is quick work, but friendship is a slow-ripening fruit. (Aristotle)

You can always tell a real friend: when you've made a fool of yourself he doesn't feel you've done a permanent job. (Laurence J. Peter)

Friendships, like marriages, are dependent on avoiding the unforgivable. (John D. MacDonald)

True friendship is like sound health, the value of it is seldom known until it be lost. (Charles Caleb Colton)

Giving

All day long he craves for more, but the righteous give without sparing. (Proverbs 21:26)

Give, and it will be given to you. A good measure, pressed down, shaken together and running over, will be poured into your lap. For with the same measure that you use, it will be measured to you. (Luke 6:38)

If there be any truer measure of a man than by what he does, it must be by what he gives. (Robert South)

It is not what you keep, but what you give that makes you happy. (Benjamin E. Mays)

Make it a rule in everything you do, give people more than they expect to get. (David Joseph Schwartz)

Remember this: Whoever sows sparingly will also reap sparingly, and whoever sows generously will also reap generously. Each man should give what he has decided in his heart to give, not reluctantly or under compulsion, for God loves a cheerful giver. (2 Corinthians 9:6-7)

When we eat out, most of us expect to tip the waiter or waitress fifteen percent. When we suggest ten percent as a minimum church offering, some folks are aghast. (Felix A. Lorenz)

You can give without loving, but you cannot love without giving. (Amy Carmichael)

The dead carry with them to the grave in their clutched hands only that which they have given away. (DeWitt Wallace)

When it comes to giving, some people stop at nothing. (Unknown)

Giving is a very good criterion, in a way, of a person's mental health. Generous people are rarely mentally ill people. (Dr. Karl Menninger)

A man there was and they called him mad; the more he gave the more he had. (John Bunyan)

Humor

A boy becomes an adult three years before his parents think he does, and about two years after he thinks he does. (General Lewis B. Hershey)

American people could always be counted on to do the right thing — after they have exhausted every other alternative. (Winston Churchill)

Bless those who curse you. Think what they would say if they knew the truth. (Mother Teresa)

Everything is funny as long as it's happening to somebody else. (Will Rogers)

For a marriage to be peaceful the husband should be deaf and the wife blind. (Unknown)

I know God won't give me anything I can't handle. I just wish He didn't trust me so much. (Mother Teresa)

The alarm clock was invented by the Devil in order to prevent anyone from being happy for more than twenty-four hours in a row. (Marilyn vos Savant)

I think it's good to learn from your mistakes; but I'm getting tired of learning something new every day. (Tom Wilson)

If a man could have half his wishes, he would double his troubles. (Benjamin Franklin)

In China we can criticize Darwin but not the government. In America you can criticize the government but not Darwin. (Chinese Paleontologist)

Life is like a roll of toilet paper. The closer it gets to the end, the faster it goes. (Andy Rooney)

I never let my schooling interfere with my education. (Mark Twain)

They say hard work never hurt anybody, but I figure why take the chance? (Ronald Reagan)

Joy

A cheerful heart is good medicine, but a crushed spirit dries up the bones. (Proverbs 17:22)

Man is fond of counting his troubles but he does not count his joys. If he counted them up as he ought to, he would see that every lot has enough happiness provided for it. (Fyodor Dostoevsky)

The opposite of joy is not sorrow. It is unbelief. (Leslie Weatherhead)

The joy of a good man is the witness of a good conscience; have a good conscience and thou shalt have gladness. (Thomas à Kempis)

Possessing God's power enables us to face life with enthusiasm; it gives us a deep inward peace because we are not afraid of tomorrow. There comes into our lives an inner joy that outward circumstances cannot reach. Because God is within us, and because God is love, there flows out from us a love for others that sweeps away all prejudice, jealousy, and hate. (Charles L. Allen)

Joy is found in obedience. (Richard J. Foster)

Restore to me the joy of your salvation, and grant me a willing spirit, to sustain me. (Psalm 51:12)

Though the fig tree does not bud and there are no grapes on the vines, though the olive crop fails and the fields produce no food, though there are no sheep in the pen and no cattle in the stalls, yet I will rejoice in the Lord, I will be joyful in God my Savior. (Habakkuk 3:17-18)

This is the day the Lord has made; let us rejoice and be glad in it. (Psalm 118:24)

No man truly has joy unless he lives in love. (St. Thomas Aquinas)

Kindness

Every passing day is one that is gone forever. Make sure it is one in which you have done something for others, especially those who cannot do for themselves. (Sierra Breeze)

Do unto others as you would have others do unto your children. (Dr. Edwin Leap)

He who sees a need and waits to be asked for help is as unkind as if he had refused it. (Dante)

I shall pass through this world but once. Therefore, if there be any kindness I can show or any good thing I can do, let me do it now for I shall not pass this way again. (Etienne de Grellet)

You cannot do a kindness too soon, for you never know how soon it will be too late. (Ralph Waldo Emerson)

You catch more flies with honey than with vinegar. (Henri IV of France)

Ask any decent person what he thinks matters most in human conduct: five to one his answer will be "kindness." (Lord Kenneth Clark)

No act of kindness, no matter how small, is ever wasted. (Aesop)

One kind word can warm three winter months. (Unknown)

The best portion of a good man's life is his little nameless, unremembered acts of kindness and love. (William Wordsworth)

Three things in human life are important: the first is to be kind; the second is to be kind; and the third is to be kind. (Henry James)

Neighbor

Do not waste your time bothering about whether you love your neighbor; act as if you did.... When you are behaving as if you love someone, you will presently come to love him. (C. S. Lewis)

He who despises his neighbor sins, but blessed is he who is kind to the needy. (Proverbs 14:21)

I tell you the truth, whatever you did for one of the least of these brothers of mine, you did for me. (Matthew 25:40)

It is one of the most beautiful compensations in life that one cannot sincerely try to help another without helping himself. (Ralph Waldo Emerson)

Therefore each of you must put off falsehood and speak truth-fully to his neighbor, for we are all members of one body. (Ephesians 4:25)

Love your neighbor, yet pull not down your hedge. (Unknown)

These are the things you are to do: Speak the truth to each other and render true and sound judgment in your courts; do not plot evil against your neighbor, and do not love to swear falsely. (Zechariah 8:16-17)

Love your neighbor as yourself. (Matthew 22:39)

You're never quite sure how you feel about a neighbor until a "For Sale" sign suddenly appears in front of his house. (O. A. Battista)

We can love our neighbors without necessarily liking them. In fact, liking them may stand in the way of loving them by making us overprotective sentimentalists instead of reasonably honest friends. (Frederich Buechner)

We have committed the Golden Rule to memory; let us now commit it to life. (Edwin Markham)

Optimism

A pessimist sees the difficulty in every opportunity; an optimist sees the opportunity in every difficulty. (Winston Churchill)

An optimist is a person who sees a green light everywhere, while the pessimist sees only the red stop light.... But the truly wise person is color-blind. (Albert Schweitzer)

An optimist is one who makes the best of it when he gets the worst of it. (Laurence J. Peter)

Being an optimist after you've got everything you want doesn't count. (Kin Hubbard)

I am an optimist. It does not seem too much use being anything else. (Winston Churchill)

I ... have been described as an undying optimist, always seeing a glass half full when some see it as half empty. And, yes, it's true — I always see the sunny side of life. And that not just because I've been blessed by achieving so many of my dreams. My optimism comes not just from my strong faith in God, but from my strong and enduring faith in our country. (Ronald Reagan)

Sow your seed in the morning, and at evening let not your hands be idle, for you do not know which will succeed. (Ecclesiastes 11:6)

Let other pens dwell on guild and misery. (Jane Austen)

Positive anything is better than negative nothing. (Elbert Hubbard)

The pessimist is the man who believes things couldn't possibly be worse, to which the optimist replies, "Oh, yes, they could." (Vladimir Bukovsky)

Worry less about cholesterol and more about gratitude, forgiveness and optimism. We need to see the glass as half-full, not half-empty. (Dr. George E. Vaillant)

Prayer

I can always pray for someone when I don't have the strength to help him in some other way. (Andy Rooney)

If we pray for help to do the next right thing, everything will turn out the way it should. (Dick Feagler)

Therefore confess your sins to each other and pray for each other so that you may be healed. (James 5:16)

A man who is intimate with God will never be intimidated by men. (Leonard Ravenhill)

The best way to get to know a new friend is to spend time with him, to talk with him. And the best way to get to know God better is to spend time with Him, to talk to Him. That's what prayer is — simply talking to God. (Stephen L. Spanoudis)

Give us the strength to encounter that which is to come. (Robert Louis Stevenson)

Is prayer your steering wheel or your spare tire? (Corrie ten Boom)

There is no part of religion so neglected as private prayer. (J. C. Ryle)

It is possible to offer fervent prayer even while walking in public or strolling alone, or seated in your shop ... while buying or selling ... or even while cooking. (John Chrysostom)

Neglect of prayer is one great cause of backsliding. (J. C. Ryle)

The prayer that says it all.... Thank you. (Dan Taddeo)

Just pray for a tough hide and a tender heart. (Ruth Graham)

We must lay before Him what is in us, not what ought to be in us. (C. S. Lewis)

Quarrel

A foolish son is his father's ruin and a quarrelsome wife is like a constant dripping. (Proverbs 19:13)

As charcoal to embers and as wood to fire, so is a quarrelsome man for kindling strife. (Proverbs 26:21)

At least 99 percent of the time, quarrels start over petty, unimportant matters. (David Joseph Schwartz)

Better a dry crust with peace and quiet than a house full of feasting with strife. (Proverbs 17:1)

Like one who seizes a dog by the ears is a passer-by who meddles in a quarrel not his own. (Proverbs 26:17)

It is to a man's honor to avoid strife, but every fool is quick to quarrel. (Unknown)

It takes two to make a quarrel. (Unknown)

People generally quarrel because they cannot argue. (G. K. Chesterton)

Pride only breeds quarrels, but wisdom is found in those who take advice. (Proverbs 13:10)

Quarrels would not last so long if the fault were on only one side. (Francois de la Rochefoucauld)

Starting a quarrel is like breaching a dam; so drop the matter before a dispute breaks out. (Proverbs 17:14)

And the Lord's servant must not quarrel; instead, he must be kind to everyone, able to teach, not resentful. (2 Timothy 2:24)

Religion

But if we have faith in Jesus Christ and believe in the Lord God, we will seek to do his will, act, and leave the consequence to Him. (Benjamin E. Mays)

Christianity is different from all other religions. They are the story of man's search for God. The Gospel is the story of God's search for man. (Dewi Morgan, rector)

No man is really free who is afraid to speak the truth as he knows it, or who is too fearful to take a stand for that which he knows is right. (Benjamin E. Mays)

Religion is caught, not taught. (W. R. Inge)

Religion is the everlasting dialogue between humanity and God. (Franz Werfel)

Religion that God our Father accepts as pure and faultless is this: to look after orphans and widows in their distress and to keep oneself from being polluted by the world. (James 1:27)

The heart of Religion is not an opinion about God, such as philosophy might reach as the conclusion of an argument; it is a personal relation with God. (William Temple)

We have just enough religion to make us hate, but not enough to make us love one another. (Jonathan Swift)

Science without religion is lame, religion without science is blind. (Albert Einstein)

It is better to follow even the shadow of the best than to remain content with the worst. And those who would see wonderful things must often be ready to travel alone. (Henry van Dyke)

Frequently, religion has met with hostility on college campuses. But when it takes many students three quadruple espressos and unknown quantities of Prozac to get through the day, it's evident they need something more. (Naomie Schaefer Riley, author)

Self

A person's attitude toward himself has a profound influence on his attitude toward God, his family, his friends, his future, and many other significant areas of his life. (Bill Gothard)

If I long to improve my brother, the first step toward doing so is to improve myself. (Christina Rossetti)

Make the most of yourself, for that is all there is to you. (Ralph Waldo Emerson)

One should examine oneself for a very long time before thinking of condemning others. (Molière)

The true value of a human being can be found in the degree to which he has attained liberation from the self. (Albert Einstein)

Where religion goes wrong it is because, in one form or another, men have made the mistake of trying to turn to God without turning away from self. (Aelred Graham)

If you really want insight about yourself, ask someone you know, trust, and respect. (Daniel Taddeo)

Self-reflection is the school of wisdom. (Baltasar Grecian, 1647)

He who falls in love with himself will have no rivals. (Benjamin Franklin)

Temptation

Blessed is the man that perseveres under trial, because when he has stood the test, he will receive the crown of life that God has promised to those who love him. (James 1:12)

Do not be harsh with others who are tempted, but console them as you yourself would wish to be consoled. (Thomas à Kempis)

Many a dangerous temptation comes to us in fine gay colors that are but skin-deep. (Matthew Henry)

No temptation has seized you except what is common to man. And God is faithful; he will not let you be tempted beyond what you can bear. But when you are tempted, he will also provide a way out so that you can stand up under it. (1 Corinthians 10:13)

So long as we live in this world we cannot escape suffering and temptation. (Thomas à Kempis)

Watch and pray so that you will not fall into temptation. The spirit is willing, but the body is weak. (Matthew 26:41)

We make a huge spiritual leap forward when we begin to focus less on beating temptation and more on avoiding it. (Bruce Wilkinson)

What makes resisting temptation difficult, for many people, is that they don't want to discourage it completely. (Franklin P. Jones)

When Satan knocks, I just send Christ to the door. (Billy Graham)

When temptation calls you on the phone, don't argue with it. Just hang up. (Pastor Rick Warren)

Understanding

A fool finds no pleasure in understanding but delights in airing his own opinions. (Proverbs 18:2)

A man of knowledge uses words with restraint, and a man of understanding is even-tempered. (Proverbs 17:27)

Be not disturbed at being misunderstood; be disturbed rather at not being understanding. (Chinese Proverb)

Buy the truth and do not sell it; get wisdom, discipline and understanding. (Proverbs 23:23)

Blessed is the man who finds wisdom, the man who gains understanding. (Proverbs 3:13)

He who gets wisdom loves his own soul; he who cherishes understanding prospers. (Proverbs 19:8)

He who ignores discipline despises himself, but whoever heeds correction gains understanding. (Proverbs 15:32)

Tell me; and I'll forget. Show me; I may not remember. Involve me; and I'll understand. (Benjamin Franklin)

To know a little less and to understand a little more; that, it seems to me, is our greatest need. (James Ramsey Ullman)

Wisdom is supreme; therefore, get wisdom. Though it cost all you have, get understanding. (Proverbs 4:7)

Grieve not that men do not know you; grieve that you do not know men. (Confucius, 500 BC)

Virtue

A general dissolution of principles and manners will more surely overthrow the liberties of America than the whole force of the common enemy. While the people are virtuous they cannot be subdued; but when once they lose their virtue they will be ready to surrender their liberties to the first external or internal invader.... If virtue and knowledge are diffused among the people, they will never be enslaved. This will be their great security. (Samuel Adams)

Love is the highest virtue. (Martin Luther)

The first step to virtue, is to love virtue in another man. (Thomas Fuller)

Virtue is not to be considered in the light of mere innocence, or abstaining from doing harm; but as the exertion of our faculties in doing good. (Samuel Butler)

All virtue is loving right, all sin is loving wrong. (Hubert van Zeller)

Search others for their virtues, thyself for thy vices. (Benjamin Franklin)

Virtue does not consist so much in abstaining from vice, as in not having an affection for it. (W. T. Eldridge)

When we are planning for posterity, we ought to remember that virtue is not hereditary. (Thomas Paine)

A timid question will always receive a confident answer. (Lord Darling)

Frequently noted virtues in the Bible: forgiveness, goodness, gratitude, honesty, kindness, thankfulness, and understanding. (Daniel Taddeo)

Wisdom

A wise man makes his own decisions, an ignorant man follows public opinion. (Unknown)

A wise man may look ridiculous in the company of fools. (Unknown)

Be wiser than other people if you can, but do not tell them so. (Earl of Chesterfield)

Common sense in an uncommon degree is what the world calls wisdom. (Samuel Taylor Coleridge)

He is a wise man who does not grieve for the things which he has not, but rejoices for those which he has. (Epictetus)

From the errors of others a wise man corrects his own. (Publius Syrus)

Where there is a feast of words there is often a famine of wisdom. (St. Catherine of Siena)

Wisdom consists of the anticipation of consequences. (Norman Cousins)

The art of being wise is the art of knowing what to overlook. (William James)

The next best thing to being wise oneself is to live in a circle of those who are. (C. S. Lewis)

Wisdom is the highest virtue, and it has in it four other virtues; of which one is prudence, another temperance, the third fortitude, the fourth justice. (Boethius)

It is far easier to be wise for others than to be so for oneself. (Francois de la Rochefoucauld)

If any of you lacks wisdom, he should ask God, who gives generously to all without finding fault, and it will be given to him. (James 1:5)

The wisest man is generally he who thinks himself as the least so. (Nicolas Boileau Despreaux)

Worldliness

Are you not ashamed of heaping up the greatest amount of money and honour and reputation, and caring so little about wisdom and truth and the greatest improvement of the soul? (Socrates, 468-399 BC)

Do we, first and foremost, belong to this world, where the priorities are wealth and power and success, where celebrities are the rulers? (Pastor Kelly Peters)

Do not conform any longer to the pattern of this world, but be transformed by the renewing of your mind. (Romans 12:2)

Worldliness corrupts and absolute worldliness corrupts absolutely. But it is not something invented by the affluent society. It goes back to the Garden of Eden. The material thing is given first place. (Hubert van Zeller)

Worldly people harden under adversity; unworldly people, more ready to accept, become more flexible. The world does not like being shaped according to God's plan; the spirit does. (Hubert van Zeller)

Love to God will expel love to the world; love to the world will deaden the soul's love to God. (Octavius Winslow)

The world has forgotten, in its preoccupation with left and right, that there is an above and below. (Franz Werfel)

Unless there is within us that which is above us, we shall soon yield to that which is about us. (Peter Taylor Forsyth)

We can love the world, or love God. We cannot love both God, who is eternal, and the world, which is transitory. (St. Augustine)

Don't be squeezed into the mold of this world. (Romans 12:2)

If you keep in step with God, you will be out of step with the world. (Unknown)

Youth

Almost everything that is great has been done by youth. (Benjamin Disraeli)

Don't laugh at a youth for his affectations; he is only trying on one face after another to find a face of his own. (Logan Pearsall Smith)

Our youth now love luxury. They have bad manners, contempt for authority; they show disrespect for their elders, and love chatter in places of exercise. They no longer rise when elders enter the room. They contradict their parents, chatter before company, gobble up their food and tyrannize their teachers. (Socrates, 468-399 BC)

In case you're worried about what's going to become of the younger generation, it's going to grow up and start worrying about the younger generation. (Roger Allen)

The right way to begin is to pay attention to the young, and make them just as good as possible. (Plato)

The young always have the same problem — how to rebel and conform at the same time. They have now solved this by defying their parents and copying one another. (Quentin Crisp)

Young people are thoughtless as a rule. (Homer)

Young people ought not to be idle. It is very bad for them. (Margaret Thatcher)

Oh, to be only half as wonderful as my child thought I was when he was small, and only half as stupid as my teenager now thinks I am. (Rebecca Richards)

Youth looks forward, middle-age merely looks startled, and old age looks back. (Lord Mancroft)

Matters that Matter, Volume I

Introduction

The purpose of this section is to identify what eminent thinkers have to say about life and to help people better prepare themselves and their families to maximize their lives.

The 4,000 notable quotables that appear on these pages are far from exhaustive. However, they are, in my opinion, quotations that speak to the broadest scope of life with fewest words, from pre-birth to death and everything in between.

Matters that Matter is an insightful and concise collection of quotes that focus on all the important aspects of living. It is through these priceless thoughts from an array of figures in history that the reader will come to terms with what truly matters in life.

It is my belief that the ten chapters with 900 relevant subject topics, arranged alphabetically and indexed for easy reference, will truly fertilize your mind, and cultivate your life to the fullest.

— Dan Taddeo

A random selection arranged alphabetically follows:

Aging

In every age the "good old days" were a myth. No one ever thought they were good at the time. For every age has consisted of crisis that seemed intolerable to the people who lived through them. (Brooks Atkinson)

Age is strictly a case of mind over matter. If you don't mind, it doesn't matter. (Jack Benny)

Age is a bad traveling companion. (English Proverb)

Growing old isn't so bad when you consider the alternative. (Maurice Chevalier)

Older people who are physically active are less likely to become depressed and feel isolated. (Colin Milner, International Council on Active Aging)

Never grow so old that you cannot change your mind. (Unknown)

Oftener than not the old are uncontrollable; their tempers make them difficult to deal with. (Euripides, 425 BC)

At my age, when I order a three-minute egg, they ask for the money up front. (Milton Berle)

Do not regret growing older. It is a privilege denied to many. (Unknown)

One secret of growing old gracefully is never to lose your enthusiasm for meeting new people and seeing new places. (Unknown)

The worst thing about growing old is listening to your children's advice. (Unknown)

Experience is a comb which nature gives us when we are bald. (Chinese Proverb)

Let every year make you a better person. (Benjamin Franklin)

Old age is not a total misery. Experience helps! (Euripides, 410 BC)

I warmed both hands before the fire of life; it sinks, and I am ready to depart. (Walter Savage Landor, 1849)

Appearance

Even though most things are far different from what they appear, a good exterior is the best recommendation of the excellence of the interior. (Baltasar Grecian)

Why not be oneself? That is the whole secret of a successful appearance. If one is a greyhound why try to look like a Pekinese? (Edith Jitwell)

While we look at outward appearances, the Lord looks at hearts (our inner disposition and character). (1 Samuel 16:7)

The face is the mirror of the heart. (Japanese Proverb)

Most of us mask our true identity to ourselves and the world, thus depriving us of a fulfilling life that includes the kind of relationships with God and others we are meant to have. This behavior is attributed to today's emphasis on appearance. (Bill Thrall, author)

How anybody dresses is indicative of his self-concept. If students are dirty and ragged, it indicated they are not interested in tidying up their intellects either. (S. I. Kayakawa, President of San Francisco State College)

Of all the things you wear, your expression is the most important. (Unknown)

Someone who looks slovenly probably doesn't care about himself or other people. (Sam Fulwood, columnist)

Never judge from appearance. (Jonathan Swift)

Change

All changes, even the most longed for, have their melancholy; for what we leave behind us is part of ourselves; we must die to one life before we can enter into another. (Amatole France)

Change is the law of life and those who look only to the past or the present are certain to miss the future. (John F. Kennedy)

Even in slight things the experience of the new is rarely without some stirring of foreboding. (Eric Hoffer)

For something new to emerge into the world something old has to die. (Pastor Kelly Peters)

Nothing will ever be attempted if all possible objections must first be overcome. (Samuel Johnson)

There is nothing permanent except change. (Heraclitus, 475 BC)

One of the most difficult things to accept, particularly for the old, is change. Change should be seen not as accidental to life but as part of life itself. (Hubert van Zeller)

We must adjust to changing times and still hold to unchanging principles. (Jimmy Carter)

Everyone thinks of changing the world, but no one thinks of changing himself. (Leo Tolstoy)

Lord, when we are wrong, make us willing to change. And when we are right, make us easy to live with. (Peter Marshall)

The world hates change, yet it is the only thing that has brought progress. (Charles F. Kettering)

Be the change you want to see in the world. (Mohandas K. Ghandi)

Christianity

All 123 of the first 123 colleges founded in America were founded by Christians for Christian purposes. The idea of the university was born in the bosom of the church. (Dr. Paul Maier)

Christ has been the greatest benefactor to the human race the world has ever known. (D. James Kennedy, Ph.D.)

Christianity is a thing of unspeakable joy, but it begins, not in joy, but in wretchedness. And it does no good to try to get to the joy by bypassing the wretchedness. (C. S. Lewis)

Christianity is not a religion but a relationship of love expressed toward God and man. (Sherwood Eliot Wirt)

Christianity has not been tried and found wanting; it has been found difficult and not tried. (G. K. Chesterton)

If you have no joy in your religion, there's a leak in your Christianity. (W. A. [Billy] Sunday)

No one is without Christianity, if we agree on what we mean by the word. It is every individual's individual code of behavior by means of which he makes himself a better human being than his nature wants to be than if he followed his nature only. (William Faulkner)

Religion is based upon what we do, Christianity is based upon what Christ has done. (Greg Albrecht)

The Catholic must adopt the decision handed down to him; the Protestant must learn to decide for himself. (Rousseau)

The exclusive claims of Christianity: one God, one Savior, one Truth, one People, and one Way. (The Bible)

The most prevalent failure of Christian love is the failure to express it. (Reverend Paul E. Johnson)

If Christianity is false, it is of no importance. If Christianity is true, it is of infinite importance. The one thing it cannot be is of moderate importance. (C. S. Lewis)

Conduct

Brighten the corner where you are. (Old Proverb)

Holy living consists in doing God's work with a smile. (Mother Teresa)

Do not withhold good from those to whom it is due when it is in the power of your hand to do so. (Proverbs 3:26)

Live in each season as it passes; breathe the air, drink the drink, taste the fruit, and resign yourself to the influence of each! (Henry David Thoreau)

Delight in the other person's success as much as you do in your own. (Daniel Taddeo)

People spend too much time finding other people to blame, too much energy finding excuses for not being what they are capable of being, and not enough energy putting themselves on the line, growing out of the past, getting on with their lives. (J. Michael Straczynski)

If you would be interesting, be interested; if you would be pleased, be pleasing; if you would be loved, be lovable; if you would be helped, be helpful. (William Arthur Ward)

The true measure of a man is how he treats someone who can do him absolutely no good. (Samuel Johnson)

An eye for an eye makes the whole world blind. (Unknown)

I believe that every right implies a responsibility; every opportunity, an obligation; every possession, a duty. (John D. Rockefeller Jr.)

These are the things that you shall do: speak the truth to one another, render in your gates judgments that are true and make for peace, do not devise evil in your hearts against one another. (Zechariah 8:16-17)

What a wonderful life I've had! I only wish I'd realized it sooner. (Colette)

Death

Death sneaks up on you like a windshield sneaks up on a bug. (Unknown)

If we live, we live to the Lord; and if we die, we die to the Lord. So, whether we live or die, we belong to the Lord. (Romans 14:8)

If you aren't fit to face death today, it's very unlikely you will be by tomorrow; besides, tomorrow is an uncertain quantity; you have no guarantee that there will be any tomorrow for you. (Thomas à Kempis)

Those who believe heaven is a real place makes a big difference on how they view death. (Daniel Taddeo)

To think of death and to prepare for death is not a surrender. It is a victory over fear. (Paul Wilhelm von Keppler)

When you accept that you can die at any time, you focus on the essentials. Once you learn how to die, you learn how to live. (Morrie Schwartz, on his death bed)

He hath lived ill that knows not how to die well. (Thomas Fuller, M.D.)

It hath often been said, that it is not death but dying, which is terrible. (Henry Fielding)

Let us endeavor so to live that when we come to die even the undertaker will be sorry. (Mark Twain)

Neither the sun nor death can be looked at steadily. (La Rochefoucauld)

Death is just a distant rumor to the young. (Andy Rooney)

Democracy

A democracy is predicated on the idea that ordinary men and women are capable of governing themselves. (Adolf Berle)

Democracy does not guarantee equality of conditions — it only guarantees equality of opportunity. (Irving Kristol)

It has been said that democracy is the worst form of government except for all the others that have been tried. (Sir Winston Churchill)

It's a republic if you can keep it. (Benjamin Franklin)

One of the evils of democracy is you have to put up with the man you elect whether you want him or not. (Will Rogers)

Self-government requires qualities of self-denial and restraint. (John F. Kennedy)

The real democratic American idea is not that every man shall be on a level with every other man, but that every man shall have liberty to what God made him, without hindrance. (Henry Ward Beecher)

There can be no daily democracy without citizenship. (Ralph Nader)

Well-educated citizens should be capable of defending their own liberty or taking on the burden to defend the liberty of those who can't defend their own. (Michael Schwartz, president of Cleveland State University)

Divorce

Because divorce has become so common, the whole world has downplayed the toll a divorce takes on kids. (Gregory Keck, psychologist)

Divorces fail as well as marriages. (Unknown)

Divorce is as difficult, or more so, for children to cope with than the death of a parent. (Daniel Taddeo)

Divorce lingers forever with children. (Gary Chapman)

Do not compare your mate with anyone else, for there is danger in becoming discontent by comparing your partner with others. (Nick Holly)

Emotional divorce precedes actual divorce. (Unknown)

In divorce situations: a few are better off, a few are even worse off (especially financially), and the vast majority end up exchanging one set of problems for another. (Daniel Taddeo)

It is very difficult and expensive to undo after you are married the things that your mother and father did to you while you were putting your first six birthdays behind you. (Bureau of Social Hygiene Study)

Many marriages are destroyed each year in America by financial worries created by debt and poor money management. (Larry Burkett, author)

People wouldn't get divorced for such trivial reasons, if they didn't get married for such trivial reasons. (Unknown)

Second marriages have a higher failure rate than the first time down the aisle. (Lyric Wallwork Winik)

There are four minds in the head of a divorced man who marries a divorced woman. (Palestinian Talmund, 400 BC)

You can't escape marital stress the way you can other types of stress. Most people think marriage as a comfort zone and a place where you can relax, but when that is stressed, there is no safe haven. (Professor Ann Marie Cans)

Freedom

America will remain the land of the free so long as it is the home of the brave. (Elmer Davis)

Everyone is in favor of free speech. Hardly a day passes without it being extolled, but some peoples' idea of it is that they are free to say what they want but if anyone says anything back, that is an outrage. (Sir Winston Churchill)

Freedom can't be bought for nothing. If you hold her precious, you must hold all else of little worth. (Seneca, 100 AD)

Freedom of speech means that you shall not do something to people either for the views they have, or the views they express, or the words they speak or write. (Hugo Black)

I disapprove of what you say, but I will defend to the death your right to say it. (Voltaire)

Free people are free to be wise and to be unwise. That's part of what freedom is. (Donald Rumsfeld, Secretary of Defense)

If a nation values anything more than freedom, it will lose its freedom, and the irony of it is that if it is a comfort or money that it values more, it will lose that too. (W. Somerset Maugham)

In the true sense freedom cannot be bestowed, it must be achieved. (Franklin D. Roosevelt)

{On Ancient Athens}: In the end, more than freedom, they wanted security. They wanted a comfortable life, and they lost it all: security, comfort, and freedom. When the Athenians finally wanted not to give to society but for society to give to them, when the freedom they wished for most was freedom from responsibility then Athens ceased to be free and was never free again. (Edward Gibbon)

The liberty of the individual must be thus far limited: he must not make himself a nuisance to other people. (John Stuart)

Those who expect to reap the blessings of freedom must, like men, undergo the fatigue of supporting it. (Thomas Paine, 1776)

Freedom is never license to do as we please, but only to do as we ought. (Lord Acton)

A train is free to travel only when it stays on the tracks. (Daniel Taddeo)

God

God does not promise us happy endings in a world where laws of nature and human cruelty take their daily toll; God's promise is not that we will be safe, but that we will never be alone. (Rabbi Harold S. Kushner)

God doesn't call the qualified, he qualifies the called. (Greg Albrecht)

God is looking for obedience, not just good intentions. (Unknown)

God is real, no matter how you feel. (Rick Warren, pastor)

God never asks about our ability or our inability — just our availability. (Unknown)

One on God's side is a majority. (Wendell Phillips)

No matter how good we are, God could love us no more, and no matter how bad we are, He could love us no less. His love is prompted by nothing we do. (Mike Huckabee)

The Lord is not slow in keeping his promise, as some understand slowness. He is patient with you, not wanting anyone to perish, but everyone to come to repentance. (2 Peter 3:9)

We don't change God's message; His message changes us. (Unknown)

We have been born under a monarchy; to obey God is freedom. (Seneca, 100 AD)

We know that all things work together for good to those who love God. (Romans 8:28)

With God there is no mutual ground; one chooses to be Godly or worldly. (Reverend Daniel Wegrzyn)

Government

Our constitution was made only for a moral and religious people. It is wholly inadequate to the government of any other. (John Adams)

Our government is a government of the people, by the people, and for the people. (Abraham Lincoln)

The modern state no longer has anything but rights; it does not recognize duties anymore. (George Bernanos, 1955)

The responsibility of great states is to serve and not to dominate the world. (Harry Truman, 1945)

The state is the servant of the citizens and not his master. (John F. Kennedy)

Too often individuals turn to the government for solutions that the government cannot provide without lessening our personal liberty. (Matthew Abens)

Too often our Washington reflex is to discover a problem and then throw money at it, hoping it will somehow go away. (Senator Kenneth B. Keating)

We have staked the whole of our political institutions upon the capacity of mankind for self-government, upon the capacity of each and all of us to govern ourselves, to control ourselves, to sustain ourselves according to the Ten Commandments of God. (James Madison, Chief Architect of the Constitution)

Whenever you have an efficient government you have a dictatorship. (Harry Truman)

It is the duty of all nations to acknowledge the providence of Almighty God, to obey His will, to be grateful for His benefits, and humbly implore His protection and favor. (George Washington, 1789)

Our best protection against bigger government in Washington is better government in the states. (Dwight Eisenhower)

Those who will not be governed by God, will be ruled by tyrants. (William Penn)

Health

For the best physical and mental health: socialize, optimize, and exercise (SOE). (Dr. Mark Frankel, M.D.)

Healthy eating habits, exercise, and weight management are the keys to long-term health, happiness, and life span. (Tara Parker-Pope, *Wall Street Journal*)

If you're healthy, you're a millionaire. (Polish Proverb)

Only after seeing one go quickly from good to poor health and death can one appreciate one's own health. (Daniel Taddeo)

New research suggests that prolonged stress reduces our ability to fend off infectious diseases. (Dr. Isadore Rosenfeld, M.D.)

People need rest, good food, fresh air and exercise — the quadrangle of health. (William Oslet)

People who are always taking care of their health are like misers who are hoarding a treasure which they have never spirit enough to enjoy. (Lawrence Sterne)

The most powerful and dangerous problem in health care today is denial. Everybody looks around and says, "It's not going to be me." (Dr. Steven Nissen, cardiologist)

The trouble about always trying to preserve the health of the body is that it is so difficult to do without destroying the health of the mind. (G. K. Chesterton)

We are not sensible of the most perfect health as we are of the least sickness. (Montaigne)

When we are well, we all have good advice for those who are ill. (Terence, 166 BC)

Husband & Wife

And let us consider how we may spur one another toward love and good deeds. (Hebrews 10:24)

A perfect husband is one who doesn't expect a perfect wife (and vice versa). (Daniel Taddeo)

Better to live on a corner of the roof than share a house with a quarrelsome wife [husband]. (Proverbs 21:9)

Between a man and his wife nothing ought to rule but love. (William Penn)

Blessed are the husband and wife who are as polite and courteous to one another as they are to their friends. Blessed are those mates who never speak loudly to one another, and who make their home a place "where seldom is heard a discouraging word." (Unknown)

Disrespect for women has invariably been the surest sign of moral corruption. (Baron Montesquieu, 1748)

Husbands and wives alike think that if they simply point out their spouses' bad points often enough, their partner will gladly comply, correct their faults, and again become the perfect angels they were when dating. It never works out that way. (D. James Kennedy, Ph.D.)

So husbands ought to love their own wives as their own bodies; he who loves his wife loves himself. (Ephesians 5:28)

That we are what we are is due mostly to these two factors, mothers and fathers. (Charlotte Perkins Gilman)

These impossible women [and men]! How do they get around us! The poet was right: can't live with them, or without them. (Aristophanes, 411 BC)

When a wife or husband sins, neither is totally innocent. (Italian Proverb)

Whether women are better than men I cannot say — but I can say they are certainly no worse. (Golda Meir)

Jesus

As the centuries pass the evidence is accumulating that, measured by His effect on history, Jesus is the most influential life ever lived on this planet. (Kenneth Scott Latourette)

Christians believe "The Passion of the Christ" represents the greatest act of sacrificial love in human history: Jesus dying on the cross for the sins of all humanity. (David Briggs, *The Plain Dealer*, religion reporter)

For there is one God and one Mediator between God and men; the Man Christ Jesus. (1 Timothy 2:5)

I am the resurrection and the life. He who believes in me will live, even though he dies; and whoever lives and believes in me will never die. (John 11:25)

I am the vine, you are the branches. He who abides in Me, and I in him, bears much fruit; for without Me you can do nothing. (John 15:5)

If you seek your Lord Jesus in all things you will truly find Him, but if you seek yourself you will find yourself, and that will be your own great loss. (Thomas à Kempis)

Jesus, a man who was completely innocent, offered himself as a sacrifice for the good of others, including his enemies, and became the ransom of the world. It was a perfect act. (Mohandas K. Gandhi)

Take My yoke upon you and learn from Me, for I am gentle and humble of heart, and you will find rest for your souls. For My yoke is easy and My burden is light. (Matthew 11:29-30)

To those who hear and respond to His call, He offers the promise of grace, forgiveness, restoration, and a glorious eternity. (Dr. James Dobson)

You only love Jesus as much as the person you love the least. (Unknown)

Learning

A little learning is not a dangerous thing to one who does not mistake it for a great deal. (William Allen White)

Everything I learned about God, I've learned from the poor. (Mother Teresa)

For whatever things were written before were written for our learning, that we through the patience and comfort of the Scriptures might have hope. (Romans 15:4)

He who adds not to his learning diminishes it. (The Talmud)

I am defeated, and I know it, if I meet any human being from whom I find myself unable to learn anything. (George Herbert Palmer)

Learning is a treasure which accompanies its owner everywhere. (Chinese Proverb)

Learning is discovering that something is possible. (Unknown)

Learn to paddle your own canoe. (Unknown)

Never too late to learn. (Proverb)

One's mind is like a knife. If you don't sharpen it, it gets rusty. (Nien Cheng)

The highest goal in learning is to know God. (Unknown)

The illiterate of the twenty-first century will not be those who cannot read and write, but those who cannot learn, unlearn and relearn. (Alvin Toffler)

Liberty

If liberty means anything at all, it means the right to tell people what they do not want to hear. (George Orwell)

I know not what course others may take, but as for me, give me liberty or give me death. (Patrick Henry, 1775)

Let every nation know, whether it wishes us well or ill, that we shall pay any price, bear any burden, meet any hardship, support any friend, oppose any foe, in order to assure the survival and success of liberty. (John F. Kennedy)

Liberty is always dangerous, but it is safest thing we have. (Reverend Harry Emerson Fosdick)

The independence and liberty you possess are the work of joint counsels and joint efforts, of common danger, suffering and successes. (George Washington, 1776)

The shallow consider liberty a release from all laws, from every constraint. The wise see in it, on the contrary, the potent Law of Laws. (Walt Whitman, 1881)

The thing they forget is that liberty and freedom and democracy are so very precious that you do not fight to win once and stop. (Sergeant Alvin C. York)

The tree of liberty must be refreshed from time to time with the blood of patriots and tyrants. (Thomas Jefferson)

Life

Whatever is at the center of your life is your God. (Pastor Rick Warren)

The best portion of a good man's life is his little, nameless, unremembered acts of kindness and love. (William Wordsworth)

Life is a mirror: if you frown at it, it frowns back; if you smile, it returns the greeting. (Thacheray)

One of the tragedies of life is that once a deed is done, the consequences are beyond our control. (Benjamin E. Mays)

Life is what happens to you while you're busy making plans. (John Lennon)

We don't see things as they are, we see them as we are. (Anais Nin)

Nobody can ruin your life if you don't let them. (Joyce Meyer, speaker)

Life is hard by the yard; but by the inch, life is a cinch. (Unknown)

Look at life through the windshield, not the rearview mirror. (Unknown)

The secret of life: do something for somebody else. (Unknown)

Life is a coin. You can spend it any way you wish, but you can only spend it once. (Unknown)

Life is 10% what happens to you, 90% how you respond to it. (Charles Swindoll, pastor)

The measure of a life is not its duration but its donation. (Corrie ten Boom)

Life was not given to be used up in the pursuit of what we must leave behind us when we die. (Joseph May)

Manhood: Husbands & Fathers

Masculinity ought to be defined in terms of relationships and taught in terms of the capacity to love and be loved. (Joe Ehrmann, football coach)

Athletic ability, sexual conquest, and economic success are not the best measurements of manhood. (Joe Ehrmann, football coach)

A father holds awesome power in the lives of his children, for good or ill. Families have understood that fact for centuries. (Dr. James Dobson)

Don't make a baby if you can't be a father. (New York City Board of Education)

Fathers, do not provoke your children, lest they become discouraged. (Colossians 3:21)

It behooves a father to be blameless if he expects a son to be. (Homer, 1000 BC)

Greatness of name in the father often times overwhelms the son; they stand too near one another. The shadow kills the growth. (Ben Johnson, 1640)

Husbands, love your wives and do not be harsh with them. (Colossians 3:19)

The most important thing a father can do for his children is to love their mother. (Theodore Hesburgh)

This is what a father ought to be about: helping his son to form the habit of doing right on his own initiative, rather than because he's afraid of some serious consequences. (Terence, 160 BC)

You don't raise heroes, you raise sons. And if you treat them like sons, they'll turn out to be heroes, even if it's just in your own eyes. (Walter Schierra Sr., astronaut)

Marriage

A family based on marriage between a man and a woman was a pillar of society that justly had rights and duties specific to it. (Pope John Paul II)

It is a fusion of two hearts — the union of two lives — the coming together of two tributaries, which after being joined in marriage, will flow in the same channel in the same direction... carrying the same burdens of responsibility and obligation. (Peter Marshall, pastor)

It is not marriage that fails; it is people that fail. All that marriage does is to show them up. (Reverend Harry Emerson Fosdick)

A man who marries a woman to educate her falls a victim to the same fallacy as the woman who marries a man to reform him. (Elbert Hubbard)

Remember, all marriages have stormy periods. Seek professional help. Eighty-six percent of unhappy couples who stick it out report being much happier five years later. (Linda Waite)

The goal of every married couple, indeed, every Christian home, should be to make Christ the Head, the Counselor and the Guide. (Paul Sadler)

To keep your marriage brimming with love in the loving cup,

whenever you're wrong, admit it; whenever you're right, shut up. (Ogden Nash)

Marriages, like the people in them, are not perfect and take work. I believe you should always work toward these two goals: 1.) overcoming your own weakness; but 2.) allowing your spouse to have them. The goals may be unreachable, but if both husband and wife aim for them, they will become better people and avoid damaging their love relationship in the process. (Marilyn vos Savant)

Couples can improve their relationship beyond belief if they can convince themselves that their partner, as a package, is equal to or greater than themselves. (Daniel Taddeo)

There is no more lovely, friendly, and charming relationship, communion, or company than a good marriage. (Martin Luther)

There is nothing nobler or more admirable than when two people who see eye to eye keep house as man and wife, confounding their enemies and delighting their friends. (Homer, 1000 BC)

Success in marriage does not come merely through finding the right mate, but through being the right mate. (Barnett Brickner)

Components of a good marriage: mutual respect, genuine commitment, good communications, time and effort, spiritual unity. (*The Billy Graham Christian Worker's Handbook.*)

Mistake

A man who has committed a mistake and doesn't correct it is committing another mistake. (Confucius, 500 BC)

Convert mistakes into learning opportunities. (Daniel Taddeo)

Learn from mistakes of others; you can't make them all yourself. (Unknown)

Measure twice, cut once. (An old carpenter's saw)

Manage mistakes by learning to play within your abilities and realizing that managing and minimizing mistakes in life is critical. (Jack L. Groppel, Ph.D.)

Sulking about your mistakes only leads to future ones. (Bill Rancic)

When in doubt, cut the piece of wood long and the piece of iron short. (Carmine Taddeo)

You may never make a discovery if you're afraid to make a mistake. (Unknown)

Remember your mistakes just long enough to profit by them. (Dan McKinnon)

A thousand mistakes are an education if you learn something from every one. (Unknown)

I think it's good to learn from your mistakes; but I'm getting tired of learning something new every day. (Tom Wilson)

Morality

How is it that nobody has dreamed up any moral advances since Christ's teaching? (Michael Green)

Morality is not taught, but caught, from the prevailing moral culture. (Daniel Griswold, The Cato Institute)

The only immorality is to not do what one has to do when one has to do it. (Jean Anouilh)

Whenever you are to do a thing, though it can never be known but to yourself, ask yourself how you would act were all the world looking at you, and act accordingly. (Thomas Jefferson)

We have two kinds of morality side by side: one which we preach but do not practice, and another which we practice but seldom preach. (Bertrand Russell)

Pope John Paul II accuses the media of poisoning morals, saying they often give a positive depiction of extramarital sex, contraception, abortion, and homosexuality that is harmful to society. He urges the media to promote traditional family life. 'All communication has a moral dimension. People grow or diminish in moral stature by the words which they speak and the messages which they choose to hear.' (Associated Press)

Where morality is present, laws are unnecessary. Without morality, laws are unenforceable. (Unknown)

The so-called new morality is too often the old immorality condoned. (Lord Shawcross)

Obesity

Two-thirds of Americans are overweight or obese, and the number is growing steadily. The percentage of the population that is obese has doubled since 1980; the numbers of those who are morbidly obese (100 pounds or more over the ideal weight) has quadrupled during that period. (The Centers for Disease Control)

One in three children in the USA is either overweight or at a serious risk of becoming fat. They are becoming fatter at a faster rate; the number of overweight kids between ages six and nineteen has tripled in the last thirty years. (Sharron Dalton, associate professor)

Obesity starts in the brain, not the mouth or stomach. People don't overeat because they're hungry, but as a way of meeting their emotional needs and making it through the day. (Diane Hales, editor and author)

New evidence shows that a major cause of the obesity epidemic is the pattern of desk jobs, car pools, suburban sprawl, and other environmental and lifestyle factors that discourage physical activity. (Rob Stein, *Washington Post*)

The double cheeseburger: a weapon of mass destruction. (Ralph Nader)

To be thinner people have to make permanent changes. (Dr. James Jill, University of Colorado)

Because obesity is a worldwide epidemic, the Cleveland Clinic has opened a new weight management center. Studies will address such questions as "Why do some people become obese and some don't?" and "Why does obesity cause diabetes?" (Dr. Philip Schauer, the Clinic's new director of advanced laparoscopic and bariatric surgery)

Opportunity

Opportunity doesn't even need to knock if you just leave your door open. (Tom Wilson)

A wise man will make more opportunities than he finds. (Francis Bacon)

It is better to be prepared for an opportunity and not have one than to have an opportunity and not be prepared. (Whitney Young Jr.)

If opportunity doesn't knock, build a door. (Joe Mazur)

Opportunities are usually disguised as hard work, so most people don't recognize them. (Ann Landers)

Great opportunities may come once in a lifetime, but small opportunities, such as acts of telling the truth, being kind, and encouraging others, surround us every day. (Pastor Rick Warren)

When one door closes another door opens; but we so often look so long and so regretfully upon the closed door that we do not see the ones which open for us. (Alexander Graham Bell)

Opportunity seldom knocks twice. (Proverb)

Therefore, as we have opportunity, let us do good to all people, especially to those who belong to the family of believers. (Galatians 6:10)

Opportunity may knock once, but temptation bangs on your front door forever. (Unknown)

People usually do their best under the circumstances they find themselves at that particular point in time. (Daniel Taddeo)

Perseverance

Most of the important things in the world have been accomplished by people who have kept on trying when there seemed to be no help at all. (Dale Carnegie)

Perseverance can tip the scales from failure to success. (Unknown)

Press on. Nothing in the world can take the place of persistence. (Ray A. Kroc, McDonald's Corporation)

'Tis a lesson you should heed, try, try again. If at first you don't succeed, try try again. (William Edward Hickson)

Throw your heart over the fence and the rest will follow. (Norman Vincent Peale)

When you get to the end of your rope, tie a knot and hang on. (Franklin D. Roosevelt)

Perseverance is more prevailing than violence; and many things which cannot be overcome when they are together, yield themselves up when taken little by little. (Plutarch, 100 AD)

Nothing of great value in life comes easily. (Norman Vincent Peale)

Great works are performed not by strength, but by perseverance. (Samuel Johnson)

There are only two creatures that can surmount the pyramids: the eagle and the snail. (Eastern Proverb)

Trying times are no time to quit trying. (Unknown)

Perseverance is a great element of success. If you only knock long enough and loud enough at the gates, you are sure to wake up somebody. (Henry Wadsworth Longfellow)

Sin

Anyone, then, who knows the good he ought to do and doesn't do it, sins. (James 4:17)

As Christians we know that Jesus took the punishment for our sins onto Himself and therefore God will not punish us for specific sins. However, we must remember that sin often has consequences that God does not remove. (Fred Grundmann, author)

Every thought, word, and deed contrary to God's Law is sin; that every human being is a sinner by birth; that all evil in the world is the consequence of man's sinning. (Martin Luther)

He who conceals his sins does not prosper, but whoever confesses and renounces them finds mercy. (Proverbs 28:13)

Jesus is the atoning sacrifice for our sins, and not only for ours but also for the sins of the whole world. (1 John 2:2)

No matter how many new translations of the Bible come out, the people still sin the same way. (Unknown)

Sins cannot be undone, only forgiven. (Igor Stravinsky)

Sin is disobedience of God. (Pastor Charles Stanley)

The acts of the sinful nature are obvious: sexual immorality, impurity, and debauchery; adolatry and witchcraft; hatred, discord, jealousy, fits of rage, selfish ambition, dissensions, factions, and envy; drunkenness, orgies, and the like. I warn you, as I did before, that those who live like this will not inherit the kingdom of God. (Galatians 5:19-21)

There is not a righteous man on earth who does what is right and never sins. (Ecclesiastes 7:20)

Success

If a man has a talent and cannot use it, he has failed. If he has a talent and uses only half of it, he has partially failed. If he has a talent and learns somehow to use the whole of it, he has gloriously succeeded and won a satisfaction and a triumph few men ever know. (Thomas Wolfe)

He who would climb the ladder must begin at the bottom. (English Proverb)

I can give you a six word formula for success: Think things through — then follow through. (Edward Rickenbacker)

It takes twenty years to make an overnight success. (Eddie Cantor)

No person can succeed without helping people. (Dr. Robert Schuller)

Secret to success: staying the course against the critics. (Jim Stevens)

Success is speaking words of praise... in cheering other peoples' ways... in doing just the best you can... with every task and every plan. (Unknown)

To be successful you must be willing to do all the things that unsuccessful people won't do. (Troy Walker, Director of Cox Communications, Cleveland)

There is no success without hardship. (Sophocles, 418 BC)

To reach the port of success we must sail, sometimes with the wind and sometimes against it — but we must sail, not drift or lie at anchor. (Oliver Wendell Holmes)

There are no shortcuts to any place worth going. (Unknown)

Success without honor is an unseasoned dish; it will satisfy your hunger, but it won't taste good. (Joe Paterno, coach)

Truth

To thine own self be true, and it must follow, as the night the day. Thou canst not then be false to any man. (Shakespeare)

To be persuasive we must be believable. To be believable we must be credible. To be credible we must be truthful. (Edward R. Murrow)

Truth and oil always come to the surface. (Spanish Proverb)

If you tell the truth you don't have to remember anything. (Mark Twain)

He that does not speak truth to me does not believe me when I speak truth. (Thomas Fuller, M.D., 1732)

The man who fears no truths has nothing to fear from lies. (Thomas Jefferson)

Pretty much all the honest truth-telling there is in the world is done by children. (Oliver Wendell Holmes)

Truth is not limited to the Scriptures, but it is limited by the Scriptures. (J. Grant Howard)

The truth is the truth, whether it is believed or not. It doesn't hurt the truth not to be believed, but it hurts you and me if we don't believe it. (George H. Hepworth)

Nearly everyone will lie to you given the right circumstances. (Bill Clinton)

Whoever can be trusted with very little can also be trusted with much, and whoever is dishonest with very little will also be dishonest with much. (Luke 16:10)

In the latter half of the twentieth century the politically correct view that all lifestyles, behaviors, and beliefs are equally valid gained acceptance and came to be known as postmodernism. If we accept postmodernism, we must conclude that there is no objective truth and that each of us are left to subjectively decide moral trust, "and everyone did what they thought was right." (Greg Albrecht)

Wealth

To acquire wealth is difficult, but to spend it wise is most difficult of all. Wealth is no insurance against discontent. (Unknown)

He is rich who hath enough to be charitable. (Sir Thomas Browne, 1642)

Riches rather enlarge than satisfy appetites. (Thomas Fuller, M.D., 1732)

The larger a man's roof, the more snow it collects. (Persian Proverb)

That glittering hope is immemorial and beckons many men to their undoing. (Euripides, 414 BC)

There is nothing wrong with people possessing riches; the wrong comes when riches possess people. (Billy Graham)

The wealthy people are those who are content with what they have. (Unknown)

Wealth brings many friends. (Proverbs 19:4)

Whoever loves wealth is never satisfied with his income. (Ecclesiastes 5:10)

For we brought nothing into the world, and we can take nothing out of it. (1 Timothy 6:7)

What good is it for a man to gain the whole world, yet forfeit his soul? Or what can a man give in exchange for his soul? (Mark 8:36-37)

If you have wealth, do not glory in it. (Thomas à Kempis)

In this world it is not what we take up, but what we give up, that makes us rich. (Henry Ward Beecher)

Womanhood: Wives & Mothers

A wife of noble character is her husband's crown, but a disgraceful wife is like decay in his bones. (Proverbs 12:4)

Be as interested in your spouse's day as you were when you were dating. (Unknown)

A mother cannot unlock all of life's doors for her children but she can help them find the keys. (Catherine Britton)

A mother's pride is a kind of milk, nourishment that can come from no other source. (Jeanne Marie Laskas)

If a woman's adult efforts are concentrated exclusively on her children, she is more likely to stifle than broaden her children's perspective and preparation for adult life. (Alice S. Rossi)

It is impossible for any woman to love her children twenty-four hours a day. (Milton R. Sapirstein)

Mothers are the most precious asset of any nation. They are more important than statesmen, than businessmen.... They have the most important occupation of any person in this nation. (Theodore Roosevelt)

She opens her mouth with wisdom, and on her tongue is the law of kindness. She watches over the ways of her household, and does not eat the bread of idleness. Her children rise up and call her blessed; her husband also, and he praises her. (Proverbs 31:26-28)

Though motherhood is the most important of all professions, requiring more knowledge than any other department in human affairs, there was no attention given to the preparation for this office. (Elizabeth Cady Stanton)

The ideal mother, like the ideal marriage, is a fiction. (Milton R. Sapirstein)

What the mother sings to the cradle goes all the way down to the coffin. (Henry Ward Beecher)

When children are little, they pull at their mother's skirt; when they grow up, they pull at their hearts. (Italian Proverb)

Work

Far and away the best prize that life offers is the chance to work hard at work worth doing. (Theodore Roosevelt, 1903)

No race can prosper till it learns there is as much dignity in tilling a field as in writing a poem. (Booker T. Washington, 1895)

When work is a pleasure, life is a joy! When work is a duty, life is slavery. (Maxim Gorky, 1903)

Work spares us from three great evils: boredom, vice, and need. (Voltaire, 1759)

The secret joy in work is contained in one word: excellence. To know how to do something well is to enjoy it. (Pearl Buck)

You're working hard to make a good life for yourself. Put at least as much effort (and more) into your spiritual life. (Daniel Taddeo)

Work is the least important thing and family is the most important. (Jerry Seinfeld)

Never leave till tomorrow what you can do today. (Benjamin Franklin)

No bees, no honey; no work, no money. (Unknown)

The only place where success comes before work is a dictionary. (Vidal Sassoon)

There can be intemperance in work just as in drink. (C. S. Lewis)

An ant on the move does more than a dozing ox. (Unknown)

We should accustom ourselves to think of our position and work as sacred and well-pleasing to God, not on account of the position and work, but on account of the word "faith" from which the obedience and work flow. (John Calvin)

Matters that Matter, Volume II

Introduction

The purpose of this section is not only to acquaint readers with the wisdom and philosophies of eminent thinkers, but also to give them a better life preparedness to maximize their potential and enjoy the experience.

Although far from exhaustive, the brief essays within these pages speak with fewest words to the broadest scope of life: before birth, the journey itself, and after death.

Matters That Matter, Volume II is an insightful and concise collection of essays that focuses on important aspects of living. These priceless thoughts from an array of historical and contemporary figures focus on what truly "matters."

I believe that the ten chapters containing 500 relevant subject topic essays arranged alphabetically and indexed for quick and easy reference will truly fertilize your mind and cultivate your life to the fullest.

— Daniel Taddeo

A random selection arranged alphabetically follows:

About Marriage

You get tested. You find out who you are, who the other person is, and how you accommodate or don't. There are a few rules I know to be true about love and marriage:

If you don't respect the other person, you're gonna have a lot of trouble.

If you don't know how to compromise, you're gonna have a lot of trouble.

If you can't talk openly about what goes on between you, you're gonna have a lot of trouble.

If you don't have a common set of values in life, you're gonna have a lot of trouble.

Your values must be alike. And the biggest one of those values is the importance of your marriage.

— *Tuesdays with Morrie* by Mitch Alborn

America

Has American society strayed from the principles upon which this nation was founded and is this cause for alarm? Historian Alexis de Tocqueville (1805-1859) once said, "America is great because America is good, and if America ever ceases to be good, America will cease to be great." General Douglas MacArthur (1880-1964) expressed his own concerns: "History fails to record a single precedent in which nations subject to moral decay have not passed into political and economic decline. There has been either a spiritual awakening to overcome the moral lapse, or a progressive deterioration leading to ultimate national disaster." Another historian, Arnold Toynbee (1889-1975), further illustrates this point: "Of the twenty-two civilizations that have appeared in history, nineteen of them collapsed when they reached the moral state America is in today."

History is filled with great civilizations that have come and gone, all experiencing moral decay from within. Historian Edward Gibbon (1737-94) listed five major causes for the decline and fall of the Roman Empire:

The rapid increase of divorce: the undermining of the dignity and sanctity of the home, which is the basis of human society.

Increasing higher taxes and the spending of public money for free bread and circuses for the populace.

The mad craze for pleasure: sports becoming every year more exciting and more brutal.

The building of gigantic armaments when the real enemy was within, the decadence of the people.

The decay of religion — faith fading into mere form — losing touch with life and becoming important to guide the people.

We need to restore the moral and spiritual values we cherish in our society — in our families, neighborhoods, schools, churches and government. *Matters That Matter, Volume II* is a call to arms to all Americans to be a part of this great challenge.

— Daniel Taddeo

Celebrating Kindness Week

Monday: Today I will not strike back. If someone is rude, impatient, or unkind, I will not respond in a like manner.

Tuesday: Today I will be careful about what I say. I will carefully choose my words, being certain that I do not spread gossip.

Wednesday: Today I will go the extra mile, I will find ways to help someone else.

Thursday: Today I will forgive. I will forgive any hurts or injuries that come my way.

Friday: Today I will do something nice for someone. I will use kind words and my smile to brighten someone's day.

— Unknown

Class

Class never runs scared. It is sure-footed and confident and it can handle whatever comes along.

Class has a sense of humor. It knows that a good laugh is the best lubricant for oiling the machinery of human relations.

Class never makes excuses. It takes its lumps and learns from past mistakes.

Class bespeaks an aristocracy unrelated to ancestors or money. Some extremely wealthy people have no class at all, while others who are struggling to make ends meet are loaded with it.

Class knows good manners are nothing more than a series of petty sacrifices.

Class is real. You can't fake it. Class never tries to build itself up by tearing others down.

Class can "walk with kings and keep its virtue and talk with crowds and keep the common touch."

Class is already up and need not attempt to look better by making others look worse. Everyone is comfortable with the person who has class because he is comfortable with himself. If you have class, you've got it made. If you don't have class, no matter what else you have, it won't make up for it.

— Ann Landers

Cold-Water Pourers

It is really very serious to observe how, even in modern times, the arts of discouragement prevail. There are men, whose sole pretense to wisdom consists in administering discouragement. They are never at a loss. They are equally ready to prophesy, with wonderful ingenuity, all possible varieties of misfortune to any enterprise that is proposed; and, when the thing is produced, and has met with some success, to find a flaw in it.

I once saw a work of art produced in the presence of an eminent cold-water pourer. He did not deny that it was beautiful, but he instantly fastened upon a small crack in it, that nobody had observed; and upon that crack he would dilate, whenever the work was discussed in his presence. Indeed, he did not see the work, but only the crack in it. That flaw, that little flaw, was all in all to him.

— Sir Arthur Helps, 1811-1873

Did You Ever Wonder Why

The sun lightens our hair, but darkens our skin?
Women can't put on mascara with their mouth closed?
You never see the headline "Psychic Wins Lottery?"
Abbreviated is such a long word?
Doctors call what they do practice?
You have to click on "Start" to stop your computer?
Lemonade is made with artificial flavor, and dishwashing liquid is made with real lemons?
The man who invests all your money is called a broker?
The time of day with the slowest traffic is called rush hour?
There isn't mouse-flavored cat food?
They're called "apartments" when they're all stuck together?
If flying is safe, they call the airport the terminal?
You park in the driveway and drive on the parkway?

— Unknown

Different Kinds of Love

The word "love" is sometimes confused with the word "like." Perhaps that is because the English language has only one word, "love," to explain a number of ideas. The Greek language, however, uses a number of terms:

Eros: Eros acts in response to an attraction in another person; it usually involves physical or sexual appeal. It is also an act of the emotions and cannot be commanded.

188

Philia: Has to do with companionship. It's often been called the "friendship" type of love.

Storge: (store-gay) Refers to love between family members.

Agape: (ah-gah-pay) This love acts in response to a need in another person. It is an act of the will, and *can* be commanded. This word is used to describe God's love for mankind, and the love people are to have for one another in response.

— Rev. Harry Wendt

Do It Anyway

People are unreasonable, illogical, and self-centered. Love them anyway.

If you do good, people may accuse you of selfish motives. Do good anyway.

If you are successful, you may win false friends and true enemies. Succeed anyway.

The good you do today may be forgotten tomorrow. Do good anyway.

Honesty and transparency make you vulnerable. Be honest and transparent anyway.

What you spend years building may be destroyed overnight. Build anyway.

People who really want help may attack you if you help them. Help them anyway.

Give the world the best you have and you may get hurt. Give the world your best anyway.

— Unknown

Each Life Affects Another's

We may not always realize that everything we do
affects not only our lives but touches others too,
for a little bit of thoughtfulness that shows someone you care
creates a ray of sunshine for both of you to share....
Yes, every time you offer someone a helping hand,
every time you show a friend you care and understand,
every time you have a kind and gentle word to give
you help someone find beauty in this precious life we live,
for happiness brings happiness, and loving ways bring love,
and giving is the treasure that contentment is made of....

— Amanda Bradley

Endurance

We are always encouraged to endure to the end, no matter what circumstances we find ourselves in. Too often we would like to just ignore that advice, because it requires an effort to be patient and not exude resistance, but show determination and stamina instead.

In all areas of our lives, we find endurance is a must and a necessity. Whether it be personally, in the circumstances of our business dealings and the people involved in these transactions, and socially; society and government must endure controlling factors as well.

If we separate each section into segments, we find going to the store or shopping indeed takes patience. We have to remain in line, go through the process of waiting our turn, and more. Heavens forbid when the person waiting on you has a problem with arithmetic if the cash register is down. Or when the person in front of you can't decide exactly what they want and heehaw around holding up the arm of progress, or can't find their wallet or credit card; this too requires endurance to keep from blowing your top.

— Laura Moore

Four Myths about Giving

Myth 1: Some people give time and some people give money.

Truth: In general, our financial contributions follow our invest-ments of time. People who give more time also give more money.

Myth 2: Money given to congregations is money not given to secular organizations or conversely, money given to other charities is money denied to congregations.

Truth: People who have learned disciplined stewardship tend to practice those disciplines in many places. Conversely, those who didn't give at the office probably are not giving anywhere else.

Myth 3: Now that so many other organizations are raising money, people aren't giving to congregations as they once were.

Truth: Overall, congregations and the programs they administer are receiving a greater share of charitable contributions.

Myth 4: Nice people finish last.

Truth: While it might make intuitive sense to think that those who cheat a little give themselves an edge, the facts of the matter appear to be more complex. A recent study has shown that ethical companies tend also to be more profit-able. It appears that those who adopt good practice in some ways tend also to adopt good practices in other ways — which leads to good performance.

— Ian Evison, Alban Research Director

Growing Older

Now Lord, you've known me a long time. You know me bet-ter than I know myself. You know that each day I am growing older and someday may even be very old, so meanwhile, please keep me from the habit of thinking I must say something on every subject and on every occasion.

Release me from trying to straighten out everyone's affairs. Make me thoughtful, but not moody, helpful but not overbearing. I've a certain amount of knowledge to share; still it would be very nice to have a few friends who, at the end, recognized and forgave the knowledge I lacked.

Keep my tongue free from the recital of endless details. Seal my lips on my aches and pains: They increase daily and the need to speak of them becomes almost a compulsion. I ask for grace enough to listen to the retelling of others' afflictions, and to be helped to endure them with patience.

I would like to have improved memory, but I'll settle for growing humility and an ability to capitulate when my memory clashes with the memory of others. Teach me the glorious lesson that on some occasions, I may be mistaken.

Keep me reasonably kind; I've never aspired to be a saint... saints must be rather difficult to live with ... yet on the other hand, an embittered old person is a constant burden.

Please give me the ability to see good in unlikely places and talents in unexpected people. And give me the grace to tell them so, dear Lord.

— Unknown

Guess Who

Can you imagine working at the following company? It has a little over 500 employees with the following statistics:

29 have been accused of spousal abuse
7 have been arrested for fraud
19 have been accused of writing bad checks
117 have bankrupted at least two businesses
3 have been arrested for assault
71 cannot get a credit card due to bad credit
14 have been arrested on drug-related charges
8 have been arrested for shoplifting
21 are current defendants in lawsuits
In 1998 alone, 84 were stopped for drunk driving.

Can you guess which organization this is? Give up? It's the 535 members of your United States Congress. The same group that perpetually cranks out hundreds upon hundreds of new laws designed to keep the rest of us in line.

— Unknown

Happiness Can Be a Mystery

Happiness is a funny thing. You can't see it or hear it or touch it and no one has ever really defined it. But those who possess it, treasure it and those who don't, often spend their lives searching for it.

Happiness comes, not from receiving, but from giving of love, of sympathy, of faith, of understanding. And, oddly enough, the more we give, the happier we become and the happier we become, the more we have to give.

Happiness is a state of mind that depends entirely on you. We talk of others "making us happy" but this is seldom the case. We make ourselves happy or unhappy by our attitudes toward ourselves, our work, our neighbors, our world.

The truly happy person is one who can be enthusiastic about the things he has to do as well as the things he wants to do.

Happiness is a wonderful thing. It is the one gift we can give ourselves — and the most precious gift that we can wish for others.

— Daniel Taddeo

Happiness Doesn't Depend on Circumstances

The happiness which brings enduring worth to life is not the superficial happiness that is dependent on circumstances. It is the happiness and contentment that fills the soul even in the midst of the most distressing circumstances and the most bitter environment. It is the kind of happiness that grins when things go wrong and smiles through tears. The happiness for which our souls' ache is one undisturbed by success or failure, one which will root deeply inside us and give inward relaxation, peace, and contentment, no matter what the surface problems may be. That kind of happiness stands in need of no outward stimulus.

— Billy Graham

How Do You Spend Your Dash?

I read of a man who stood to speak at a funeral of a friend.

He referred to the dates on her tombstone from the beginning... to the end.

He noted that first came her date of birth and spoke the following date with tears, but he said what mattered most of all was the dash between those years, 1900-1970.

For that dash represents all the time that she spent alive on earth... and now only those who loved her know what that little line is worth.

For it matters not, how much we own; the cars... the house... the cash.

What matters most is how we live and love and how we spend our dash.

So think about this long and hard... are there things you'd like to change?

For you never know how much time is left that can still be rearranged.

If we could just slow down enough to consider what's true and
real, and always try to understand how other people feel.

And be less quick to anger and show appreciation more and love
the people in our lives like we've never loved before.

If we treat each other with respect and more often wear a smile...
remembering that this special dash might only last a little
while.

So, when your eulogy is being read with your life's actions to
rehash... would you be proud of the things they say about
how you spent your dash?

— Unknown

How Kids View Parents

The most important factor in your child's self-image, says Dr.
Thomas Johnson in his book *Guidelines for Discipline*, is what he
thinks you think of him. Dr. Johnson also gives these tips:

Give attention and praise for good behavior.

Punishment should be swift, reasonable, related to the offense
— and absolutely certain to occur.

Throw out all rules you are unwilling to enforce.

Don't lecture and don't warn. Youngsters will remember
what they think is important to remember.

Don't feel you have to justify rules, although you should try
to explain them.

Don't expect children to show more self-control than you
do.

Be honest with your youngster — hypocrisy shows.

Enforce rules you really feel strongly about — no matter
what rules other parents have.

In raising children, as in everything else, what we do speaks so
much louder than what we say. Pray for the wisdom to bring
word and deed together.

— Unknown

How to Be Happy

Make up your mind to be happy. Learn to find pleasure in simple things. Make the best of your circumstances. No one has everything, and everyone has something of sorrow intermingled with the gladness of life. The trick is to make the laughter outweigh the tears.

Don't take yourself too seriously. Don't think that somehow you should be protected from misfortune that befalls other people.

You can't please everybody. Don't let criticism worry you. Don't let your neighbor set your standards. Be yourself. Do the things you enjoy doing but stay out of debt. Never borrow trouble. Imaginary things are harder to bear than real ones. Since hate poisons the soul, do not cherish jealousy, enmity, grudges. Avoid people who make you unhappy.

Have many interests. If you can't travel, read about new places. Don't hold post-mortems. Don't spend your time brooding over sorrows or mistakes. Don't be one who never gets over things.

Do what you can for those less fortunate than yourself. Keep busy at something. A busy person never has time to be unhappy.

— Robert Louis Stevenson

How to Set a Goal and Achieve It

What is a goal? Something you want to do, achieve, or obtain.

Why is a goal important? Because if you know what you want, you are more likely to get it.

Why is that? Because you will do everything you need to do to achieve your goal rather than just anything that happens to come to mind.

How can you tell when a goal is a good one? A goal is:

Measurable — so you can tell when you achieve it.

Attainable — to prevent being frustrated.

Demanding — so it is worthwhile and motivating.

Participative — so everyone who will be affected by the goal has a share in setting it.

Deadlined — so you know when to take action.

Written — so you won't forget it.

How do you set a goal?

You write it down and keep it visible, as a reminder.

You develop a plan to achieve your goal, one step at a time.

You write down checkpoints or dates on which you will compare progress with your goal. When each checkpoints date arrives, you see how well you are progressing.

— Leader's Magazine

I Believe

I believe in the supreme worth of the individual and in his right to life, liberty, and the pursuit of happiness.

I believe that every right implies a responsibility; every opportunity, an obligation; every possession, a duty.

I believe that the law was made for man and not man for the law; that government is the servant of the people and not their master.

I believe in the dignity of labor, whether with head or hand; that the world owes no man a living, but that it owes every man an opportunity to make a living.

I believe that thrift is essential to well ordered living and that economy is a prime requisite of a sound financial structure, whether in government, business or personal affairs.

I believe that truth and justice are fundamental to an enduring social order.

I believe in the sacredness of a promise, that a man's word should be as good as his bond; that character — not wealth or power or position — is of supreme worth.

I believe that the rendering of useful service is the common duty of mankind and that only in the purifying fire of sacrifice is the dross of selfishness consumed and the greatness of the human soul set free.

I believe in an all-wise and all-loving God, named by whatever name, and that the individual's highest fulfillment, greatest happiness, and widest usefulness are to be found in living in harmony with His will.

I believe that love is the greatest thing in the world; that it alone can overcome hate; that right can and will triumph over might.

— John D. Rockefeller Jr.

If I Were the Devil

I would gain control of the most powerful nation of the world;

I would delude their minds into thinking that they had come from man's effort, instead of God's blessings;

I would promote an attitude of loving things and using people, instead of the other way around;

I would dupe entire states into relying on gambling for their state revenue;

I would convince people that character is not an issue when it comes to leadership;

I would make it legal to take the life of unborn babies;

I would make it socially acceptable to take one's own life, and invent machines to make it convenient;

I would cheapen human life as much as possible so that the life of animals are valued more than human beings;

I would take God out of the schools, where even the mention of His name was grounds for a lawsuit;

I would come up with drugs that sedate the mind and target the young, and I would get sports heroes to advertise them;

I would get control of the media, so that every night I could pollute the mind of every family member for my agenda;

I would attack the family, the backbone of any nation;

I would make divorce acceptable and easy, even fashionable. If the family crumbles, so does the nation;

I would compel people to express their most depraved fantasies on canvas and movie screens, and I would call it art;

I would convince the world that people are born homosexuals, and that their lifestyles should be accepted and marveled;

I would convince the people that right and wrong are determined by a few who call themselves authorities and refer to their agenda as politically correct;

I would persuade people that the church is irrelevant and out of date, and the Bible is for the naïve;

I would dull the minds of Christians, and make them believe that prayer is not important, and that faithfulness and obedience are optional; I guess I would leave things pretty much the way they are.

— Paul Harvey

Kid-Tested Favorites

If your child says he can't find anything good to read, here is a selection of all-time bestsellers to get him or her started.

Charlotte's Web, by E. B. White
The Outsiders, by S. E. Hinton
Tales of a Fourth Grade Nothing, by Judy Blume
Shane, by Jack Schaefer
Are You There, God? It's Me, Margaret, by Judy Blume
Where the Red Fern Grows, by Wilson Rawls
A Wrinkle in Time, by Madeleine L'Engle
Island of the Blue Dolphins, by Scott O'Dell
Little House on the Prairie, by Laura Ingalls Wilder
Little House in the Big Woods, by Laura Ingalls Wilder

— *Publisher's Weekly*

Learning to Walk

At some point early in our lives, we begin to investigate our small world by crawling. As we get older, stronger, and wiser, we expand our world by learning to walk. In time, these first faltering baby steps, accomplished with many falls and bruises, lead into the steady strides that carry us through a lifetime of purposeful activities.

God expects from us what a healthy parent expects of a toddler learning to walk. He recognizes that our first steps along the path of belief will be like those of the infant trying his legs for the first time. Only with time and through His Grace and nurturing, are we able to turn those first unsteady toddler's steps into giant leaps of faith.

When you embark on a new path of faith, start with baby steps. Develop your inner strength and confidence through the tumbles and bruises that are a necessary part of growth. Make a commitment through daily prayer to get up after each fall and proceed with courage and dedication toward your goal. As children of God, we spend our lives learning to walk in the path of His Son, Jesus. Remember that He is with you and shares your excitement as you follow in His footsteps to overcome the hurdles and bars of life.

— Unknown

Listening

Effective listening is an important skill in communication and in developing and maintaining healthy interpersonal relationships.

Most of us are better at talking than listening. It takes desire and skill to hear, understand and remember what the other person is conveying to us. Body language is very important; it sometimes says what the person can't put into words. Other actions like tears, hugs, eye contact, and smiles communicate feelings, too.

Bridges in communication often vary with individuals: personal backgrounds that are similar, being in comfortable surroundings, having common interests, expressing similar ideas. Many times it's easier to communicate with someone of the same age. People who are good communicators know what they're talking about, are alert to their listener's responses and can put their message into concise words.

To be a good listener one must be patient and approachable. Allow others to have their own rights and feelings and try to see things from their point of view with an open mind. Use warm friendly tones of voice. Politeness is basic to all human relations. Help others to find their own answers and solutions rather than providing easy ones for them. Effective listening requires a willingness to make an effort and invest a little of oneself in the process.

— *Senior Hotline*, Ohio State University Extension

Out of Our Hands

Only after we begin to look back on our lives, do we realize how much time, effort, and worry we devote to things, situations, and circumstances that are out of our hands.

During our earlier years we often focus on such things as where we live, our personal appearance and trying to be something other than ourselves. During the later years the load becomes heavier and heavier with such things as will our team win, our personal health, divorce, crime, cancer, AIDS, terrorism, the economy, the threat of war and death, to name a few.

Any area of concern where we have no control over is cause for worry and becomes a "no win" situation. Only after we begin to identify and dismiss those things which are out of our hands, are we in a position to focus our time and effort toward helping to bring about positive change. This results in less worry, greater accomplishments and improved quality of life.

— Daniel Taddeo

Paradox of Our Time

The paradox of our time in history is that we have taller buildings, but shorter tempers; wider freeways, but narrower viewpoints; we spend more, but have less; we buy more, but enjoy it less.

We have bigger houses and small families; more conveniences, but less time; we have more degrees, but less sense; more knowledge, but less judgment; more experts, but more problems; more medicine, but less wellness.

We drink too much, smoke too much, spend more recklessly, laugh too little, drive too fast, get angry too quickly, stay up too late, get up too tired, read too seldom, watch TV too much, and pray too seldom.

We have multiplied our possessions, but reduced our values. We talk too much, love too seldom, and hate too often. We've learned how to make a living, but not a life; we've added years to our life, not life to years.

We've been all the way to the moon and back, but have trouble crossing the street to meet the new neighbor. We've conquered outer space, but not inner space. We've done larger things, but not better things.

These are the days of two incomes, but more divorce; of fancier houses, but broken homes. These are the days of quick trips, disposable diapers, throw away morality, one-night stands, overweight bodies, and pills that do everything from cheer to quiet, to kill.

It is a time when there is much in the show window and nothing in the stockroom; a time when technology can bring a letter to you, and a time when you can choose either to make a difference, or to just hit delete....

— Unknown

Practice the Apology

Once you realize you don't have to make yourself wrong to deliver an apology, you'll feel a new power. If you differ strongly with a friend on a political matter, you can say: "My passion for my own beliefs has made it difficult to fully understand yours. If it has caused trouble between us, I apologize. My relationship with you is far more important than whether we agree or not."

And if you have a strained situation with your boss and feel misunderstood, at least you can say, "I'm sorry for the tension that has developed between us. I intend to find a way to work it out."

If your teenage daughter screams at you that you are ruining her life with your rules, you can say, "My rules are meant to protect you and teach you how to get along with people. I'm sorry for any bossiness or coldness that I may have delivered with my message."

We cannot always act in perfect harmony with the people we love. They inevitably will feel upset, misunderstood and frustrated by things we do. But we don't have to get so caught up with figuring out who is right and who is wrong that we forget what matters. "Because of deep love, we are courageous," said the Chinese philosopher Lao-Tse more than 2,000 years ago. The power of an apology does not lie in the admission of guilt. An apology is a tool to affirm the primacy of our connection with others. It can unlock deep love in our everyday lives. Don't wait. Apologize!

— Rosamund Stone Zander, psychotherapist

Something to Laugh About

After much research, it has been discovered that the artist Vincent Van Gogh had many relatives. Among them were:

His dizzy aunt: Verti Gogh
The brother who ate prunes: Gotta Gogh
The brother who worked at a convenience store: Stopn Gogh
The cousin from Illinois: Chica Gogh
His magician uncle: Wherediddy Gogh
His Mexican cousin: Amee Gogh
The Mexican cousin's American half brother: Grin Gogh
The nephew who drove a stage coach: Wellsfar Gogh
The constipated uncle: Can't Gogh
The ballroom dancing aunt: Tan Gogh
The gay bird loving uncle: Flamin Gogh
The psychoanalyst nephew: E Gogh
The fruit loving cousin: Man Gogh
An aunt who taught positive thinking: Wayto Gogh
The little bouncy nephew: Poe Gogh
A sister who loved disco: Go Gogh
And his niece who travels the country in a van: Winnie Bay Gogh

— Dave Schwensen

The Family Is...

The family is a haven from the hurtful experiences of life. When life feels crushed and beaten, the home can be a source of help, encouragement, comfort, and guidance.

The family is the child's first learning experience. The values children learn are so important for their future.

The family is only good and helpful when each member contributes to its purposes. Where parents and children seek to be served, rather than serve, there disintegration will occur.

The family is the first place a child learns the importance of a vital faith, the inspiration of a vision and a dream, and the strength of a positive hope. All these ingredients will help.

The family is still a valued and necessary unit, despite what critics may say. The family and the home are still among our nation's most treasured possessions.

It is a major mistake to discount the family and disallow its value. It has not been proven that other forms of lifestyle can foster strengths comparable to the family.

— Neil Strait

The Importance of Manners

Manners are of more importance than laws. Upon them, in a great measure, the laws depend. The law touches us but here and there, and now and then. Manners are what vex or soothe, corrupt or purify, exalt or debase, barbarize or refine us, by a constant, steady, uniform, insensible operation, like the air we breathe in. They give their whole form and color to our lives. According to their quality, they aid morals, they supply them, or they totally destroy them.

I soon found the advantage of this change in my manners: the conversations I engaged in went on more pleasantly. The modest way in which I proposed my opinions procured them a readier reception and less contradiction. I had less mortification when I was found to be in the wrong, and I more easily prevailed with others to give up their mistakes and join with me when I happened to be in the right. And this mode, which I at first put on with some violence to natural inclination, became at length easy, and so habitual to me that perhaps for the last fifty years no one has ever heard a dogmatical expression escape me.

— Dr. Franklin

The Importance of Here and Now

In our culture, all of us are preoccupied most of the time with anticipating the future and worrying about it or with daydreaming about the past and remembering how it was. We are always trying to be happier right now, and yet much of what we do prevents us from achieving that happiness.

To be in the here and now means to be in touch with our senses, to be aware of what we are seeing, hearing, smelling, and so on. Young children find it very easy to be in the here and now; if we watch them play, we'll notice that they seldom worry about what is going to happen, an hour or two hours from now, and that they spend little time reminiscing. They are concerned with the present situation and with getting the most from it.

If, as teenagers and adults, we could be more like young children, many of the problems that bother us would disappear.

Think about how many nights we weren't able to get to sleep because we were thinking about the future or the past; how many hours of the day we wasted and how many opportunities we have missed by not allowing our mind and body to experience what is happening now. There is a saying, "The future is only a dream and the past no longer exists. The present moment is the only reality."

— Daniel Taddeo

The Importance of Work

One of the goals of parenting is to make work meaningful to children. It's very important children learn to work as soon as possible. Good work habits will help them with their schoolwork because school is work. Work teaches responsibility, a sense of accomplishment, self-satisfaction, and preparation for life. Parents should:

Assign tasks that are appropriate to age
Work along with children

Not expect perfection
Make work appear pleasant
Not pay for doing routine chores
Encourage and praise generously
Require that children do their best
Follow through with assigned tasks

The sooner parents expect responsible behavior from their children, the sooner they will come through.

— Daniel Taddeo

The Meaning of the Pledge of Allegiance to the Flag

The booklet "Flag Etiquette" published by the American Legion National Americanism Commission of Indianapolis, Indiana, shows five multinational children saluting the flag and notes that people hear and pledge a lot, but wonders if they know what it means. Then it explains:

I pledge allegiance — I promise to be true
to the flag — to the sign of our country
of the United States of America — each state that has joined to make our country
and to the republic — A republic is a country where the people choose others to make laws for them; a government that is for the people
for which it stands — the flag means the country is
one Nation — a single country
under God, indivisible — The country cannot split into parts
with liberty and justice — with freedom and fairness
for all — for each person

The pledge says you are promising to be true to the United States.

— Unknown

The Rocks in Your Life

A philosophy professor stood before his class and had some items in front of him. When class began, wordlessly he picked up a large empty mayonnaise jar and proceeded to fill it with rocks, rocks about 2" in diameter. He then asked the students if the jar was full. They agreed that it was.

So the professor then picked up a box of pebbles and poured them into the jar. He shook the jar lightly. The pebbles, of course, rolled into the open areas between the rocks. He then asked the students if the jar was full. They agreed it was.

The students laughed. The professor picked up a box of sand and poured it into the jar. Of course, the sand filled up everything else.

"Now," said the professor, "I want you to recognize that this is your life. The rocks are the important things, your family, your partner, your health, your children — anything that is so important to you that if it were lost, you would be nearly destroyed. The pebbles are the other things that matter like your job, your house, your car. The sand is everything else. The small stuff.

"If you put the sand into the jar first, there is no room for the pebbles or the rocks. The same goes for your life. If you spend all your energy and time on the small stuff, you will never have room for the things that are critical to your happiness. Play with your children. Take time to get medical checkups. Take your partner out dancing.

"There will always be time to go to work, clean the house, give a dinner party and fix the disposal. Take care of the rocks first — the things that really matter. Set your priorities. The rest is just sand."

— Unknown

Things God Won't Ask

He won't ask what kind of car you could afford to drive, but he may ask you how many people you gave a ride to church.

He won't ask you how big a house you built, but he may ask how big a church you helped build.

He won't ask you if you wore the best designer clothes, but he may ask if you ever helped clothe the needy.

He won't ask how many treasures you had on earth, but he will ask how many you laid up in Heaven.

He won't ask how big a salary you made, but he will ask how much of it you gave to further the cause of Christ.

He won't ask now many promotions you received, but he may ask how often you promoted others.

He won't ask what you did to protect your rights, but he may ask what you did to protect the rights of others.

He won't ask if you were able to live in the finest neighborhood, but he will ask if you ever tried to witness to your neighbors.

He won't ask if you received any college degrees, but he will ask if you were diligent as a student of the Bible.

He won't ask how many friends you made here, but he will ask how many of them you led to Christ.

— Unknown

The Serenity Prayer

God, grant me the serenity to accept the things I cannot change, the courage to change the things I can, and the wisdom to know the difference. Living one day at a time, enjoying one moment at a time; accepting hardship as a pathway to peace; taking, as Jesus did, the sinful world as it is, not as I would have it; trusting that you will make all things right if I surrender to Your will; so that I may be reasonably happy in this life and supremely happy with You forever in the next. Amen.

— Reinhold Niebuhr, Protestant theologian

The 7 Ups

Wake Up! Decide to have a good day. "This is the day the Lord hath made; let us rejoice and be glad in it" (Psalms 118:24).

Dress Up! The best way to dress up is to put on a smile. A smile is an inexpensive way to improve your looks. "The Lord does not look at the things man looks at. Man looks at outward appearance, but the Lord looks at the heart" (1 Samuel 16:7).

Shut Up! Say nice things and learn to listen. God gave us two ears and one mouth, so He must have meant for us to do twice as much listening as talking. "He who guards his lips guards his soul" (Proverbs 13:3).

Stand Up!... for what you believe in. Stand for something or you will fall for anything. "Let us not be weary in doing good; for at the proper time, we will reap a harvest if we do not give up. Therefore, as we have opportunity, let us do good..." (Galatians 6:9-10).

Look Up!... to the Lord. "I can do everything through Christ Who strengthens me" (Philippians 4:13).

Reach up!... for something higher. "Trust in the Lord with all your heart, and lean not unto your own understanding. In all your ways, acknowledge Him, and He will direct your path" (Proverbs 3:5-6).

Lift Up!... your prayers. "Do not worry about anything; instead pray about everything" (Philippians 4:6).

— John Ortberg

Understanding Parents

Wise children will want to please their parents. First, though, they must understand them. As any teenager knows, parents are tough to figure out. These seven tips may help:

Don't shy away from speaking their language. Try some strange-sounding words like "Let me help you with the dishes," or "Yes."

Try to understand their music. Play "When I Survey the Wondrous Cross" on the stereo until you get accustomed to the sound.

Be patient with their weaknesses. If you catch your mom sneaking a candy bar, don't jump all over her. Quietly set a good example.

Encourage your parents to talk about their problems. Keep in mind that things like earning a living or paying off the mortgage seem important to them.

Be tolerant of their appearance. When your father gets a haircut, don't try to hide him from your friends. Remember, it's important to him to look like his peers.

If they do something you think is wrong, let them know that it's their behavior you dislike, not them.

Above all, pray for them. They may seem more confident on the outside, but feel weak on the inside. They need God to get them through these difficult years.

— Haddon W. Robinson

What to Live for

To do our duty well — whatever it be, whether to sweep the streets, to saw wood, or grind knives, whatever lowliest work it be — to do it well, to do it in a sense of duty, unites us to the Highest One by a bond that nothing can break, gains us a position in the infinite spiritual universe, from which nothing can cast us down.

We may not have received ten talents, nor two, nor even one, but only a very small fraction of one. No matter, if faithful, we shall live to just as good a purpose, so far as our worthiness is concerned, as though we had a million talents and improved them all. The poorest cobbler who, in a dutiful spirit, out of love to God and man, does the work of his calling, is just as acceptable as the righteous ruler of the greatest kingdom on the earth, just as acceptable as the highest archangel that stands before the Throne of the universe, or flies on flaming wings to carry the orders of his Sovereign to the armies of Heaven that have their stations among the stars.

— C. S. Henry

When You Thought I Wasn't Looking

When you thought I wasn't looking, I saw you hang my first painting on the refrigerator, and I wanted to paint another one.

When you thought I wasn't looking, I saw you feed a stray cat, and I thought it was good to be kind to animals.

When you thought I wasn't looking, I saw you make my favorite cake for me, and I knew that little things are special things.

When you thought I wasn't looking, I heard you pray, and I believed there is a God I could always talk to.

When you thought I wasn't looking, I felt you kiss me good night, and I felt loved.

When you thought I wasn't looking, I saw tears come from your eyes, and I learned that sometimes things hurt, but it's all right to cry.

When you thought I wasn't looking, I saw you give to someone needy and I learned the joy of giving.

When you thought I wasn't looking, I saw you always did your best and it made me want to be all that I could be.

When you thought I wasn't looking, I heard you say "thank you" and I wanted to say thanks for all the things I saw when you thought I wasn't looking.

— Unknown

Winners and Losers

Executives' Digest has published some thoughts about winners and losers that are worth thinking about:

The winner is always a part of the answer; the loser is always a part of the problem.

The winner says, "Let me do it for you"; the loser says, "That's not my job."

The winner sees an answer for every problem; the loser sees a problem in every answer.

The winner sees a green near every sand trap; the loser sees two or three sand traps near every green.

The winner says, "It may be difficult but it's possible"; the loser says, "It may be possible but it's too difficult."

You can't "win 'em all." But you can choose to be a winner rather than a loser. A winner accepts defeat, gets up, and goes on.

The difference is attitude. And we're not stuck with our attitudes. We learned them; we can "unlearn" them. "It may be difficult, but it's possible."

— Unknown

The Benediction

The Lord bless you and keep you;

The Lord make His face shine upon you,

and be gracious to you;

The Lord lift up His countenance upon you and [grant]

you peace. Amen.

— Numbers 6:24-26

WORDS OF WISDOM /
WORDS OF WISDOM, TOO

Words of Wisdom
A1-55673-995-8 / 56pgs / 5x7 / $4.95

Words of Wisdom, Too
A0-7880-0936-2 / 248pgs / 4.375x7 / $9.95

ONE NATION WITHOUT GOD
*Facing The Consequences Of A Society That
No Longer Values Choosing Right From Wrong*

A0-7880-1632-6 / 80pgs / 5.25x8.25 / $6.95

BACK TO BASICS
Parenting Principles: A Biblical Perspective

A1-55673-546-4 / 148pgs / 5.5x8.5 / $7.95

SCRIPTURE SERVINGS
FOR SPIRITUAL STRENGTH

A0-7880-2058-7 / 380pgs / 5.5x8.5 / $9.95

NOTABLE QUOTABLES
3,000 Quotations From A To Z

A1-59185-216-1 / 256pgs / 5.5x8.5 / $12.95

MATTERS THAT MATTER
VOL. 1 AND 2
*Guaranteed To Fertilize Your Mind
And Cultivate Your Life*

Matters That Matter, Volume 1
A1-60002-011-9 / 460pgs / 6x9 / $16.95

Matters That Matter, Volume 2
A1-59453-758-5 / 392pgs / 6x9 / $14.95